WRITE to PUBLISH

By

Donald L. Boone

INTRODUCTION

If, you purchase this book to learn to write correct English, or any other language for that matter, or perhaps to improve your spelling, even your Grammar, you will be in error as this book contains little along those lines. This book is being offered to help develop your need to convey the written word to the reading public, or those of your choosing.

So, if it has come about that you've decided you want to be a writer? Well, Learning to write is not a piece of cake, but it can be fun. In fact, writing is probably the hardest thing for the human mind to do. Learning to write, can at times, seem to be an awesome undertaking. Authors are not born as authors, they have to learn how to write just like the rest of us. Remember you build a book one paragraph at a time. The reason for this book is to help you choose a writing direction. Perhaps to motivate your thought processes into actually producing something, regardless of its content, or intent.

Writing is very rewarding, and in many cases, very profitable. The only real hurdle in the publishing world is in accepting the fact that you will meet with rejection. This will come through rejection letters from editors. You can expect them until you practice your writing skills enough to suit their needs. If you do not accumulate rejection letters, you are not writing.

There are writers who think aggressively, those who think with passion, some reason things out on a logical basis. There are some who think well into the future, and rarely in the here and now. There are those writers who insist that their words end up on the best seller list, and consequently, because of this attitude, may give up before any thing of value is accepted by the publishing world.

I cannot make you a writer. You are either a writer, or you're not. I can only teach you writing tips and tricks. You can only find out about your skills if you try your hand at writing.

TABLE of CONTENTS

COMMON ERRORS

Every writer makes errors and it is often the same error time after time. This is one of the reasons it is so hard for a writer to edit their own work. Yet, for beginning writers, the errors are often simplistic. Whereas, if the writer will compare what they write, to the material they read, they should notice the differences.

Consider the following portion of a story. A simple children's story, and the common error.

☆

CHILDREN OF THE RAINBOW.

It was a very long time ago, and in a distant land I am told. It seems there was a small village about two or three miles, from Queen Judith's castle. The countryside provided good crops for the people of the village, and Queen Judith looked after the people who lived in her Queendom. She took great care to see that they were all in good health, and had plenty of food to eat. Near the village, and close to their farmland, were many caves to be found. Caves that no one had ever explored before. One year, while the people from the village were out in the fields gathering their crops for the coming winter months, some children came out of one of the caves and began to walk about in the fields. Children none of the village people had ever seen before. But, the appearance of these children seemed strange, because the children were all different colors. As

1

they walked around in the fields, it appeared as though they were in a trance, as if they were walking in their sleep. In the beginning, it frightened the villagers, but they overcame their fears, and took the children back to the village with them. When they tried to get the children to eat porridge and bread, they would not eat. Not knowing what to do, the villagers led the children to Queen Judith's castle, and the good Queen was surprised at how the children looked. One girl, who was three, was yellow, as were her eyes, her hair, her skin and her clothes. Another girl, now four years old, was orange. Of course her Skin, her hair, her eyes, and her clothes were the same color. The next girl, now five years old, was red, and she, like the others had hair, eyes, clothes, and skin that was all red. The six year old girl was green, and the eight year old girl was purple.

✭

You can see how hard this story portion is to read; yet, this is exactly how many writers write in the beginning. Everything gets lumped together as they move along in their story line. However, if it is separated into paragraphs, with the dialog separated, it is much easier to read, and to follow the story as it unfolds.

While reading the different versions and portions of this story, just think about your own writing, is it page after page of continuos text. Lacking paragraphs, and separated dialog, or have you written it carefully.

Now here's the same story, but written differently.

CHILDREN OF THE RAINBOW.
It was a very long time ago, and in a distant land I am told. It seems there was a small village about two or three miles, from Queen Judith's castle. The countryside provided good crops for the people of the village, and Queen Judith looked after the people who lived in her Queendom. She took great care to see that they were all in good health, and had plenty of food to eat.

Near the village, and close to their farmland, were many caves to be found. Caves that no one had ever explored before. One year, while the people from the village were out in the fields gathering their crops for the coming winter months, some children came out of one of the caves and began to walk about in the fields. Children none of the village people had ever seen before.

But, the appearance of these children seemed strange, because the children were all different colors. As they walked around in the fields, it appeared as though they were in a trance, as if they were walking in their sleep.

In the beginning, it frightened the villagers, but they overcame their fears, and took the children back to the village with them. When they tried to get the children to eat porridge and bread, they would not eat.

Not knowing what to do, the villagers led the children to Queen Judith's castle, and the good Queen was surprised at how the children looked. One girl, who was three, was yellow, as were her eyes, her hair, her skin and her clothes.

Another girl, now four years old, was orange. Of course her Skin, her hair, her eyes, and her clothes were the same color.

The next girl, now five years old, was red, and she, like the others had hair, eyes, clothes, and skin that was all red. The six year old girl was green, and the eight year old girl was purple.

When the good Queen found out the children had refused to eat, she had an idea. She knew the children had come at harvest time, so she tried something different. She offered cooked yellow corn to the yellow girl, and the yellow girl ate the corn quickly.

Then the Queen offered a cooked orange pumpkin to the Orange girl, and she too, ate her fill.

The red girl ate tomatoes, the green girl ate green beans, and the purple girl ate purple grapes.

Two days after the girls were taken to the castle, a big storm started. The wind howled, and made shrieking noises as it found its way through cracks and crevices in the old castle walls.

The wind blew so hard, it pushed the doors to the castle wide open, and when the doors were open, the wind began to stop.

When the wind stopped, the rain started. Yet, in the distance, anyone who looked could see the Sun beginning to shine. When this happened, the children suddenly stood up in the castle courtyard, and began to walk outside leaving the castle's walls behind.

When they were all outside, and in the open, the village people, and the Queen, watched as the children walked into the last of the raindrops, and this was just before the Sun crowded the rain out of the way for the day.

The children began to dance and jump high, then higher, and higher, and can you guess what happened? The last drops of rain turned several colors, and a rainbow lifted them high into the sky, then set them down in a far distant land.

After that, every year at the end of harvest season, a rainbow would visit the village, as if saying "Thank you."

✫

The error of course is to be found in the first part of this example. It is simply that the text runs on and on without any white space. A continuous ongoing block of wording tends to lose the reader attention. Should they stop reading for any reason, it becomes a problem trying to figure out where they are leaving off, and where it is they are to begin when they come back to the story. Make it easy for your reading public and give them a place to stop and come back to easily.

The question is this. Why would such seemingly simple errors be made by writers of today? The answer is often found in our reading habits. According to Alex F. Osborn's book of 'How to become more creative,' he states that after people leave school, only 52% of us, as adults, read books.

Reading is like vitamins for your mind. If you don't read, odds are you will not write correctly. Writing and reading go hand in hand. Often a writer will emulate their favorite writer, sometimes following a similar writing pattern in their own writing lives.

On the subject of dialog, which is better, saying "I explained it to her," or actually telling her with dialog, and why.

A story line should contain 23% - 35% dialog. It is easier for the reader to follow the story, and you need the words.

If a reader has trouble following, or understanding what you have written, you are not writing correctly.

SPELLING AND GRAMMAR.

Of course spelling, and grammar are topics we will discuss, though many of us do not like to think of how badly we may be at either subject.

A topic that now comes into play, and one that can help a writer immensely, are the available computer software programs for writers. As a writer in today's world, if you are not using a computerized word processor, you are putting a tremendous restriction on your writing ability. To a degree that you may not be able to compete with other writers fighting for a place in the publishing world.

Nearly every word processing program contains a spell checker, which will check every word as you write it on the printed page. However, a spell checker will not tell you if you have used the correct word in the correct place, only if it is spelled correctly. With this in mind, the following sentences will illustrate examples of the kinds of things that can happen.

'The boat was not there's to use.' Appears correct to a spell checker, but it is not correct.

The correct wording, 'The boat was not theirs to use.' Also appears as correct.

Another example is 'She would go on this trip, weather he went along, or stayed home.'

Instead of, 'She would go on this trip, whether he went along, or stayed home.'

Most spell checker programs will offer the writer several choices of words to choose from. This list stems from the potential possibilities that your misspelled word might fit into those it finds listed in your software program. From this list, you have only to choose the correct word and to have it replace the incorrect one in your line of text.

Yet, there will be times, when the word you really need is not found in the list being presented to you. Now you have a problem, you will have to actually get out your dictionary to find the correct spelling. However, you may also have the ability to add words added to your spell checker list in the computers dictionary.

Grammar problems often involve the simple words that are used in error, such as 'its and it's. Perhaps 'lay, lie, laid' is one of your problems; as they are for most writers.

KEEPING SENTENCES SHORT

It is easy to go on and on in a sentence, it can go as if it has no end in sight, almost to the point of its becoming boring to the reader, yet containing information that can be useful in some manner to someone for some reason, at some time.

This first sentence contains 51 words. Why not just say, long sentences can be boring, yet informative.

Quite often in newspapers, you will find one sentence is also a paragraph. At the most, a newspaper paragraph may include two sentences.

You can write long sentences, but your written work should also have short sentences to help balance out the material for the reader.

Short sentences are so easy to read that a writer can often get away with writing errors, as they go un-noticed. However, I am not telling you that you can write short sentences and produce lousy writing, because you can't.

If you write sentences in excess of twenty words, you are restricting your chances of gaining a wide readership. This includes editors. The normal sentence is fifteen to twenty words per sentence. How short can they be, well as short as you want to write them and still get the meaning across.

Of course, you can't write a lengthy manuscript using only short sentences. You will have to offset your prose with some long sentences.

Quite often, a longer sentence uses more words than is necessary to get the point across, as in the following.

'Applications from four departments for financial assistance in development training programs were voted approval by the board of directors.'

It could be said as simply. 'The directors granted four departments money for training programs.'

The difference is ten words.

The question is this, How often will you read a book that contains long, long sentences, from start to finish. Once, maybe.

If you are a writer of long sentences, you will stop this style of writing, about the same time you finlsh writing your second book. Of course, the first book will still be sitting on a shelf waiting for some editor to accept it the way it is written.

As you write, any sentence that runs over two lines should be reviewed for excess words. Unless it is a fragmented sentence, sometimes these work well, though writing teachers will discourage their use.

Sometimes a fragmented sentence will get a meaning across without all of the proper wording, such as in dialog.

FAMILIAR WORDING

For a writer who wants to communicate facts and ideas to others, familiar wording is required. The wise writer will use big words sparingly, so as not to impede his or her meaning. Short words are part of the solid foundation; large words are often too complicated for many individuals. To use large words on a reading audience is to show off some kind of knowledge, or lack thereof. It may, in the long run, turn readers against your writing.

To get your message across quickly and easily, use the words that are more familiar to the general readership. Yes, you do need a large vocabulary, but you need to discipline yourself in its use. A wise man once said. "Big men use little words; little men use big words."

In a sense, it's getting social, and speaking as you would normally speak to others.

THE FIVE W's

An often overlooked method of covering all of your bases when writing, is the use of the five 'W's' rule. These are actually quite simple to do, but can be easily omitted. The order in which they are used is not important, only the usage.

WHO - the story is about, is important to the reader.

WHAT - is happening in the story?

WHY - the story is being told.

WHERE - is the story taking place?

WHEN - is the event taking place?

WHO the story is about, often falls into place naturally, as does the reason WHY it is taking place in the person's life. It is WHAT, and WHEN it is happening, that gets easily overlooked. In the writer's mind, he/she understands what is going on, but he/she often forgets that the reader does not know WHERE it's happening.

13

In your story lines, remember you also need some tension in a story to keep a reader reading. This is brought about with a degree of UNCERTAINTY, EMOTION, and reader INVOLVEMENT.

In your areas of UNCERTAINTY, as soon as one problem is taken care of, a new one should take place. Also, the main character must care in some manner. The reader needs to care also.

WRITING STYLES

DESCRIPTIVE WRITING.
This kind of writing takes place in novels, short stories, and poetry. This type of writing is used to create a picture for the reader to see in their minds' eye. To see, to hear, to feel, and to bring about a response. This is how you bring your characters into the story piece by piece. A tidbit here, and a tidbit there until the reader understands each character. This is what you do to let the reader see the view out of the window, the flat tire, etc. Descriptive writing is saying what you see.

Any writing must pull the reader into the story (hooking them) and leaving them wondering, waiting and wanting to understand what is about to happen next.

CREATIVE WRITING.

Creative writing is when you just sit down to write without planning what it is you really want to produce on the printed page. Perhaps you have a general idea in mind, but nothing planned. When you start, the writing flows easily as it comes out of your mind and fills pages of paper.

It's common for this kind of writer to be working away, and suddenly find themselves saying. "How in the world did that happen?" Suddenly, the author may even discover that the main character in the story has done something totally unexpected, surprising even to the author.

Some writers feel they have to make a story outline of what they want each chapter to be about, what each character needs to do, how to act, the character's feelings, or family background. Most creative writers do not bother with this kind of preparation, they just write. However, should you feel the need to make a story outline, by all means do so.

It's a tough thing to do, that is the leaving out any words that are not necessary in the story.

Perhaps I should say, 'The hard thing to do, is omitting un-necessary words.'

COMBINATIONS OF EXPOSITORY & CREATIVE WRITING.

In the most successfully written fiction stories, you will find these two types of writing go hand in hand. Do not start a story strictly with an exposition, start it with a section of creative writing. Once you have the reader hooked, you can begin to use sections of expository writing to explain things, or conditions. You must keep the reader interested in reading the story line, but you must also explain why, or how some things are in place and how they work.

When you first start writing fiction, remember the following tips.

The description of your story is done in a matter of steps; you don't have to start showing things, or telling about things in the story, just start writing.

Exposition writing is the best way to convey information that sets up a scenario. It's the best way to provide abstract, or unfamiliar information.

However, when you start your story, don't start with exposition, you need to be dramatic in the opening. Use whatever it takes. Dialog, descriptions, a character's thoughts, anything to hook the reader into reading the entire story.

The exposition style of writing helps control the pace of your story, using it in varying portions, gives your readers a mixture of showing and telling.

You must also remember that the end of your story is why the reader has been reading. So when you get to the end, make it climactic. Again use whatever you have too, thoughts, feelings, dialog, action, or descriptions. Do whatever you need to do to pull the reader right into the last scene.

MEMOIRS, TRUTH OR FICTION

So, there are six of you sitting at the table. You have listened to the first three writers in your critique group, each of which has read one of the ongoing chapters of their life stories. These are memoirs for the family, now and in the future. Your eyes are open, but your creative mind has shut down. The ongoing reading of dull material has taken its toll on your conscious mind. You just can't take it anymore.

Suddenly, you are jolted back to this world, and you realize it is time to critique the last writer's work. Your head tilts toward the copy you have on the table in front of you, 'Let's see, what was this last story about.' This could be the thought that races through you mind. Somewhere along the story line, you lost all meaning of the story. Now, it is your turn to offer feedback, you may not want to be brutally honest about how exciting it was to be privileged to such wonderful writing.

In desperation, you excuse yourself to go to the bathroom. When you return, if they have not finished with the last critique, you take it upon yourself to pour everyone a fresh cup of coffee, God only knows that everyone except the reader needs it to wake up.

How far do you think a family will read through a book of memoirs written by this kind of writer? They might read the second story in desperation, and going past the third story is doubtful.

One very important item about writing Memoirs. If you write them to be self-serving, or self-pitying, even dully written, you will run into a wall. This kind of writing just doesn't go anywhere.

So, what do you do as a writer of a family history? You get realistic.

There are two ways to write Memoirs, the dull way, or the interesting way. Memoirs do not have to be one hundred percent truthful; it is okay to add a little fictional flavor.

Okay, a lot of fiction if you think you can get away with doing so, I mean if the people who you are writing about are gone, who's to say it didn't happen your way.

One more thing about writing Memoirs, it would seem odd for a life's story to be told without the complicated things that take place being included. You might be thinking, "Complications." Of course complications, no one can go through life without having some problems. Perhaps a woman has lost a child in any manner that might haunt her. This is an ongoing life complication.

Perhaps either one of a married couple has had an affair that continues to be an issue; these are complications that should be written into the memoirs as well. Life happens.

Perhaps someone under the age of eighteen has been caught shoplifting. At the time, the person involved will not think much of the event, they got caught, so? So in reality, the problems this can cause during their life, goes on for many years. The theft was only the beginning of the problems that can happen as a result of this seemingly petty crime.

In regular stories, Dialog is another tool to help move the story along. When you write your memoirs, are you just putting words on paper, or is your dialog doing something, like moving the story ever onward.

Consider the two following examples, which would you rather read about.

#1.
In the summer of 1962, I offered my sister in-law a ride to work when her car wouldn't start. After our short drive together, and the ensuing conversation, I spent time with her every summer for years.

#2.
I was to meet Marie at the bookstore as we had arranged nearly a year before. Counting down the months we had to wait until we could be together. When she arrived, she looked stunning in a lacy black dress. We spent nearly all day in bed, and we met every year for years after that.

Or which of the following.

#3.
My grandfather was involved in the import business when I was young. He seemed to make good money, and he spent lots of it on my folks.

#4.
I was to learn as an adult, that all the money my grandfather spent on his family while I was young, came from smuggling liquor into the United States from Canada. He and two other men had built a very fast boat. It looked like a regular family cruising boat, but the brass fuel tanks ran from stem to stern on both Port and Starboard sides of the hull. It had two of the biggest Marine engines available at the time.

The point is, don't write dull stuff and expect the family to read it. If it is of interest, you'll hear your relatives talking with one or another, saying something like. "Oh, sure, that really happened. The story on page 98, was a true story." Or you might hear them saying to one of the youngsters

"Don't you read the story starting on page 98. You hear me?" Of course, the child has already read that story. The other children told her about it long before.

What do you really want to pass on to your heirs, a good family history, or a dull book of facts? If some of your story lines bring a gasp, and "Oh my goodness," you can always admit to some amount of fiction, even if it isn't fiction.

NOTES:
When a good idea strikes you, you must get some kind of mental notes down on paper. Keeping a note book handy will make this easier. These notes will lead you back to the story later when you have time.

A good rule to put to use, is never quit writing at the end of a paragraph, or the end of a chapter. The best place to stop writing is in mid-sentence. Doing this will enable the mind to start right where it left off, instead of trying to start over from the beginning. If, the mind has a place already established, it will carry on easily.

HOW SHOULD CHAPTERS START?

The first chapter is the most important chapter you can write, and sometimes the hardest. It can do many things, but the most important thing it needs to do, is to pull the reader into the story. When you can do this in your first chapter, you can also sell the idea to an editor. The first chapter can open in nearly any avenue, it may be an event taking place, it can introduce any of your characters, and it may contain expository writing, creative writing, or both. What it must do, is be interesting.

The single word that fits the need here, in your first chapter, is, 'Impress.' You need to impress your reader with thoughts about the coming events. You have to suck the reader into your world of writing. You have to use what is known as a 'Hook.'

In a story, which if the following opening would you prefer to read?

#1
During your stay in the hospital, you can expect someone from the laboratory department to draw blood from your arm at the beginning of each day.

#2

It is 4 a.m., and you awake to a startling sound. It is the curtains near your bed being brushed to one side, but you swear it is the soft flutter of her wings as she approaches your bedside.

She is here for your blood, and as you shudder, your veins shrivel from fright. You know her as Lyn, but in your mind you refer to her as the "Vampire."

You see the point of the opening is easy to understand. You capture the readers reading interest. Example #2 is a portion of a published article in the Peninsula Daily News Point of View column, and appeared on the hospital's web site.

NEW CHAPTER, NEW CHARACTER.
A good practice to get into when you start a new chapter, is that you can also introduce a new character into the story line. This is not a writer's rule, it's just an easy way to get everyone in the story involved as early as possible. Don't go overboard with personal description each time, you can add material about each character from time to time as you deal with them during the story. In this manner, adding more detail as you progress will not pull the reader away from the story.

You might start out with something like this.

Claire realized early in her life that she could set herself goals and attain them. During her childhood, she tired of people continually commenting on the beauty of her light blue eyes. Only the few men in her life understood why, or when her eyes would turn to a light green.

Because of her eyes, Claire had found that when she spoke with people, she could ask them anything she wanted to ask, and because they were taken with the depth of her eyes, they would answer without thinking. Claire's eyes, became a tool for her use. Her natural ability to use her intuitive perception also helped her. She was well liked, and found doors open to her, and acceptance in places where others could not enter.

As you introduce new characters, it doesn't have to be done in every chapter until they are all known by the reader. You can put one into the story in one chapter, then perhaps two or three chapters later, you can bring another one into the story.

POLISHING THAT FIRST CHAPTER

Initially writing the first chapter to achieve perfection, then rewriting it a second time, rewriting it the third time, rewriting it the fourth time,. . . . If you do this, you are trapped. One trap a writer should avoid is this one. When you start rewriting, don't get stuck rewriting chapter one until it's perfect. Just go through a general rewrite on all of your chapters, then you can go back and start again.

Many a manuscript has been left to rot because a writer has spent such an extensive amount of time getting chapter one perfect. To the extent that they give up on the rest of the book because it is too much work.

Use some method of keeping track of your present rewriting location as you go back through your work so you don't rewrite what you've just rewritten again and again. Consider using three or four question marks or asterisks to mark the place you left off.

Sometimes it's easier to just write the entire piece, then come back and review it for writing rules that may apply. This way you'll write in your own natural writing voice. However, this may only work on short manuscripts. If you try this on book length material, and you find errors, you may have a great deal of work to do. Perhaps do it on each chapter as you finish writing.

HOW LONG IS A CHAPTER?

This can be a controversial subject, who's to say how long, or how short a chapter is to be. I have seen chapters as short as a half a page. Chapters can be anywhere from one page to a lengthy chapter of fifteen pages. A comfortable reading length is about half of that, six or seven pages.

Many new writers start out writing 250 words per double spaced page, or 500 words per single spaced page. This does not include any white space between dialog or paragraphs. This is an immediate problem for readers, there is no place to stop reading and being able to start easily again.

Most people, who read a great deal, prefer to have chapters of a length where they become easy places to stop when they tire of reading. Most readers dislike picking up the book they are currently immersed in, and having to start in the middle of a chapter. Though many have to do exactly this.

Quite often when they stop in the middle of something, they have to remember what has taken place previously. When they are about to begin reading again, they may refer back a page or two, to get back into the story line of the chapter.

The preference is, for the reader to start fresh on a new section or new chapter with new thoughts. This is also one of the reasons why the writer needs to draw them into each new chapter, then leaving the reader hanging mentally until the next chapter.

Chapters are natural breaks in the story line. A location where a writer can take license to add something which seems totally unrelated to the previous chapter, yet will be used to explain another situation that will happen later in the book.

Perhaps an "Expository subject," worked into the story line to inform and clarify something for the reader. In a sense it is like forewarning the reader. An indication that a situation of some kind will appear later in the story. A primer for something that if left unsaid, may cause the reader to question the author's work, or subject matter later in the story line.

PARAGRAPHS.

A single sentence paragraph is almost like talking, and talking is communication. It is also seduction. That's why so many people, who start the evening with dinner, and a conversation, also end up spending intimate time together.

The easiest book to read is one with short paragraphs. It might be as short as a word or two. The average paragraph is one to five sentences in length. This comes out to be about three to nine lines on the written page. Read your newspaper, you'll see that the common paragraph length is one, maybe two sentences in length.

Paragraphs should not be organized; they should be allowed to form on their own. The secret is knowing when they start, and when they stop.

Paragraphs in magazine articles should have two or three sentences, rarely four, never more. This would equal roughly six typed lines. The ending of an article must re-enforce the beginning. If your title gives one meaning, yet you deliver another, your work won't get read again.

GETTING SOCIAL

New writers have a habit of not talking to the reader. Don't avoid being sociable with those that read your writing. As a new writer, you need to be up front with the reader. Let them know what's going on right away. Don't wait until page 100 to tell them the guy died when he was seven. To be sociable, write to your readers like you speak to other people, use terms, and language your readers will understand and that will place pictures in their minds.

Don't get in the habit of dressing up the dialog language; tell it like it is. If a harried mother is, as usual, trying to do six things at once, and one of her children starts screaming from another room, she is hardly going to say, "My little darlings what can the matter be?"

She'd going to say, "Now, what the crap is goin on?"

When you can, use real people and events in your stories. Of course, you don't have to use their real names, just how they react in life. It gives the reader a feeling as if the whole story could be true. When the reader can relate to the events, they will read anything you write.

However, don't rush toward the end of your story, let it happen at its own pace. This is sometimes a problem when the writer knows the outcome or ending, before the story is completely written.

When a story is allowed to tell itself, things will fall into place naturally. The end will come when it has reached the conclusion. Don't get in a hurry to finish writing the story. I once wrote the ending to a story first. To this day, it only remains a short story and it's never been used as intended.

When you have something going on, such as a love affair, write it in such a manner that the reader can share the experience. Bring them into the bedroom with you. Let them feel the emotions. This is what your reader wants to read, not 'Dick and Jane met a the ice cream parlor, and held hands.' Okay, maybe young readers want to know about the ice cream parlor.

Readers want to feel the emotions, they want to taste that glass of wine, they want to hear the sounds, and if possible, they want to see stuff in their mind's eye. Consider if you will, what, as a reader, would you like to keep in the story, and what could you care less about. Will your reader want to know about the part you don't care for, if so, what do you do with that material.

If, while having dinner, you are talking about the latest stage play you just came from, no one cares about the red car that just drove by. You might care, but you are supposed to be writing to the reader.

There is a tendency toward using the familiar 'He thought, She thought,' wording while bringing out a character's line of thinking during a story. Doing this can stop the reader by disrupting their train of thoughts.

One way around this problem is to produce their thoughts without drawing attention to the fact by using 'He said, she said,' wording, or by using *italics*. If, you use italics, use them sparingly. Consider the following methods of doing this.

GETTING IT ACROSS AS THOUGHTS

The usual way to write this is, Jim saw the rainbow, and he thought, 'That's pretty nice.'

Instead consider writing it this way, Jim squinted his eyes to look at the rainbow, 'That's pretty nice.'

You see the readers understand Jim is thinking this, you don't have to tell them.

Or, Jim was thinking, 'I've heard all of this before.'

It could be written as, He slumped his head forward. 'He'd heard all of this before.'

MAKING TIME CHANGES

Jim looked at the photo; he wondered how long it had been since he'd seen her.

Instead, Jim looked at the photo; She's even more beautiful than I remember. How long has it been, ten years, maybe fifteen?

MAKING DESCRIPTIONS

He liked the red dress she wore as she entered the room, he thought he'd compliment her on it.

He rubbed his eyes as she came into the room wearing a very red dress. She stood out very vividly, he would tell her how attractive she looked.

Sometimes the trick to being a successful writer, is that when you are writing to a specific audience, give them what they want to read, but give it to them in a manner that they don't expect.

To get, and keep your reader, you have to arouse their interest. You need to tease them with the story, then reward them with a solution. Arousing their interests by providing some details, which brings out questions in their minds. Use something to bait them.

WHAT TO WRITE ABOUT.
This is a question that often troubles many
writers. Writers like to write, but so what, we run
into dry spells, or what is known as writer's block.
To break through this barrier, try this. Make a list
of things you enjoy, or would like to write about
and then ask yourself, 'why'?

Perhaps, even making notes as to why you want
to write about those subjects will help. This way
you can refer back to them later. As you write,
you'll become more a polished writer, you'll
become aware of items that have a writing
market. It is a good practice to keep a notebook
with you, as idea's can arrive at strange times.

Make another list of all the things you have
knowledge of, no matter how silly they may seem.
You may be surprised to learn there are things
you know about, that others don't know, but would
like to know.

Consider writing an informational 'How-to' article,
as this is one of the easiest magazine markets to
break into, and it can be very profitable.

Write each week, no matter what else happens
you must take time to write something. Believe it
or not, most writers do not wait for inspiration,
they write to get something down on the piece of
paper in front of them. Write anything; you can
come back later to sort through it for the value.

As you write a story, explain in length about good information, or a good story line, then write shorter lengths about the bad stuff.

As a reader, think about how often you actually see material in books written in *'Italicized'* fonts. Seldom will you find passages written in this manner. The reasons are simple; it is too hard to read. It disrupts the eye, and the train of thought. Thus, it takes away from the story. However, I have found it useful to introduce, or to show a letter between two people, and on a separate page, by writing it then and changing the font used, to a script font.

Keeping it simple when writing can be easy for a polished writer, or, perhaps someone, who is used to writing. Most often they understand they have to write to a particular grade level.

Many new writers fall into the trap of trying to impress others with their knowledge through their writing. This attitude comes into play by using as many big words as possible, whereas little words will work just as well, if not better.

The writer who persists in writing above the twelfth grade level is actually telling the reader that they lack writing knowledge. It's not the same as standing up on a park bench and shouting, "I'm ignorant."

But, it's nearly the same thing. If a reader has to continually get a dictionary to look up a word you have included in your text, they won't finish reading your work.

WHO IS IT PLEASE?
The point of view used in telling a story can at first seem difficult, yet to some extent it may come to the writer naturally. Once you start a story line you can't change your mind as to the POV after you have begun to write. At least if you are well into it. It must remain the same person (first, second, or third) throughout.

FIRST PERSON is 'I or WE.'
This, the 'I' person, is the one who is narrating the story, and is active in the story. From this POV, the person telling the story, cannot tell you what someone else is thinking, they can only tell you what they think that person is thinking.

SECOND PERSON is 'You'
This can produce some odd effects. This is the writer as a second person narrating the story. It's as if 'you' the writer, are talking to someone else in the story. My telling you this information is written in the second person.

THIRD PERSON is 'He, She, It, or They'
This is the way most stories are told. It is a clear distinction between the author, and the characters. The author gets to tell everyone else what they are going to do. In this person the writer can indulge herself into the mind and thoughts of any character.

The point of view is much easier to control in the FIRST, or SECOND, But when you write in the THIRD person, you cannot forget the POV rule. If you do, you'll lose the reader.

THE WRITER'S VOICE Vs THE TEACHER'S
How should you write, your way, or the teacher's
way?

You always write your way. If a writing teacher
insists on your writing his/her way, that person is
not a good teacher. You see, when you write your
way you are using your writing voice. If the
teacher tells you to write his/her way, you are
writing with their writing voice. I have spoken with
editors who have told me they can tell which
writing students come from which writing teachers
because of the way they write.

Your writing voice is very important, because this
is what editors purchase, and what readers read.
Don't use someone else's voice. Think about it,
why do you read one writer's work over other
writers. It is because you like the way that writer
writes. With this in mind, you will understand it
when I say, "An author writes from within,"
consequently, what you read that has been written
by a particular writer, is indeed that writer. Though
you might think otherwise, this is always true.

The person, who writes from within, which is how
most writers write, is that kind of person. So, when
you read a mystery, the individual who has written
the work, is also a mystery. The writer of a
romance novel, is of course a romantic person.
Someone who writes 'How-to' is an organized
writer.

There is some truth to it when they say, "You write what you read."

WHAT KIND OF WRITER ARE YOU?

There are good writers, and there are bad writers. There are short story writers, and there are writers of novels.

Bad writers most often fade away over time. Good writers keep trying until they are successful in their quest.

At the very top of the writer's list, are the geniuses, though they may not consider themselves as such. Yet at times even they don't understand how, or why they write.

Then there are competent writers. Over time, and with lots of hard work, a competent writer can be made into a good writer.

A good writer will master the fundamentals, such as vocabulary, grammar, punctuation, and to develop their own style.

A good writer may never make a great writer.

Odds are, a bad writer cannot be made into a competent writer.

If you want to be a writer, there are two things you have to do. You have to read, and you have to write. If you don't read, you'll never be a writer, it's as simple as that.

Reading teaches you what not to do. It teaches you how to strive to be like the great writers. It teaches you styles and will lead you to discover your own style.

Can you be a writer and have an extensive social life, not likely. You may find an active social life as a serious writer, may be a thing of the past.

WRITER'S BLOCK

Writer's block is something that causes problems for most writers at one time or another, and it seems to run in cycles. Though there will be those who will argue this point. However, if you pay attention to your writing slumps, you will see they happen two or three times a year. This of course is, if you have all the free time you want for writing.

If you have children, and you want to write, this is another world to deal with. It can really help if you have a life's partner who understands your needs to becoming a writer. If you are a woman writer, this will be a partner who helps with the household chores. Though they can become a writer's widow, or widower, at least you will be at home with them.

At the same time don't lay a guilt trip on yourself, or anyone else in the family when you don't get time to write. Life happens.

Actually the best thing to do, to get over writer's block when it happens, is to write something. Anything will do the trick, just write. This might be a very good time to do a rewrite on previous work, as the material is already down on the written page.

WHAT GRADE LEVEL DO YOU WRITE AT?
Ah. . . Now there's something you may not have thought about. Yes you do need to know this valuable piece of information. Most word processors have a grammar checker that can supply you with the "Flesch-Kincaid," or similar grade level of your writing. Microsoft Word, and Word Perfect, are two of those programs, as is Grammatik. You may also hear "Grade Level," referred to as the "Fog," level.

While speaking with a writer recently, I found he insists on writing in, or about, the tenth or eleventh grade level, and then wonders why people don't like to read his material. It's because his grade writing level is over the heads of the general reading public. They simply don't understand the words he uses and are not going to keep a dictionary handy to look up the meaning of those words they are not familiar with.

If you want people to read your work, you must write to the appropriate grade level of your reading public. In the United States, the average reading grade level is grades six to nine, and most of the world is less than that.

When you think about the grade level in which you are writing, you should be aware of what level this is and to try to write to the sixth or seventh grade level.

When you start writing above that level, you restrict yourself to a smaller reading audience.

For instance on a sixth grade level the following item would read.

"I heard a hell of'a noise outside. I thought maybe a coupl'a cars ran int'a each other. When I looked outside though, I couldn't see any junk in the road."

A ninth grade level would read as follows.

"The clatter outside drew my attention. I opened the drapes, yet I could not see any carnage on the street."

To find out which level you are currently writing, check your work with a grammar checker. After you make the changes needed to your manuscript, save the results. But before you exit the program, look at the top of your work window. You should have a tool bar such as *FILE - EDIT - CHECKING PREFERENCES - STATISTICS - HELP.*

Click on *STATISTICS.* When that window drops down, click on *SHOW STATISTICS.*

Aha.... Now you see the FLESCH - KINCAID grade information. Click *NEXT* and see it all. When you are done, exit your Grammar checker program.

In Microsoft Word, choose TOOLS, then SPELLING & GRAMMAR.

In WordPerfect, choose TOOLS, GRAMMATIK, START, OPTIONS, ANALYSIS, READABILITY, then BASIC COUNTS.

This information is derived from the average amount of the words used in a sentence, and the amount of syllables per 100 words.

Most readers want to read material that is written below the twelfth grade level. Usually somewhere between the sixth and twelfth grades, is the best level's at which to write. Anything higher may require some good photographs to accompany the manuscript if you are marketing the work. The photography will sell the material, the hard to read text will not.

After the twelfth grade level of writing, that of a high school senior, the readership will drop off in droves. If you want to become a well known writer, you have to learn to write simple. Simple means just that, for and example, consider the following.

Tough reading.	**Simple reading**
The finance director related	The finance director
That substantial economies	Said that his
Are being effected in his	division is saving
division through increasing	money by sending
the time interval between	fewer questions
distributions of data	to employers.
eliciting forms to employing	
business entities.	

Ernest Hemmingway wrote at a sixth grade level, and the Wall Street journal is written on the eighth grade level.

You can write long sentences, as long as you mix in short ones as well.

Material, that is easy reading, gets read.

SELLING IT MORE THAN ONCE

Okay, you've written your query letter, and the editor replied in the positive and has asked for a hard copy. Of course when you sent the hard copy it was double-spaced, as you have become accustomed to doing it this way. After reading your hard copy, she sent you a brief note stating her offer for your work, perhaps something like the following.

"If you are in agreement, send me another hard copy, and an e-mail copy saved in rtf, or??. She might even ask for a copy on a three and a half inch diskette," saved in a compatible word processing format such as ------." Or she may just ask for a copy of your manuscript on the diskette. Odds are she will not ask for a copy on a flash drive.

"Why both," you may ask? Because two things will take place now. The editor will review the new hard copy again to see if you have made any updates to the work you previously submitted, and she will be making notes of changes she wants made as well. She will either edit your work to make the piece fit the space she has open, or because there are some changes she wants made to the manuscript. This could be some information in the work you have provided that she doesn't feel she needs for this particular publication. This could be anything, personal references, addresses, names, or whatever.

Of course she can make changes to your work, she's the editor, and if you insist on no changes being made in the way it is written, there's not much chance you'll see your work published with this editor. You'll only insist on this condition once before you find out pride is really expensive, and, of course, this editor may never bother to look at anything else you send her.

When she has finished with her changes on your hard copy, she may make the same changes on the diskette you've sent as well. Yet, she may just as well pass your hard copy and diskette along to the person who sets up the type, or printing program, and this person will then make the changes. From this point it is all handled electronically, as very little of this part of the procedure is done by hand anymore.

At the time of this writing, many editors do not require a diskette or CD copy, but it could still happen. This will present a problem for many writers who insist they don't need a word processor, or a computer word processing program.

Writers who still Insist, of which there are few, that their old typewriter has many good years left in its working ability, will find themselves left far behind with today's editors. Like it or not, the electronic age is the more solid path to the entire writing, editing, and publishing world.

If you want to be a published writer, get on the bandwagon of the electronic age. If you really don't care about being published, you can forget about buying that computer to keep up with the coming changes.

Even having a computer software program that seems to have a good, or decent word processor, may not be enough any more. Just having a word processor program will not be sufficient because with the constant changes in the magic of computers. You will need to make periodic upgrades to your software programs whether you want to or not. A word processing program that is new today, will be obsolete in about four or five years. I say about, because it can be less than that by the time you read this statement. With the electronic books being offered, you will need to be able to save files in the HTML, and PDF formats as well.

To stay current with your publisher, and editor, you will need to have an up to date word processor. Up to date means a word processor that the editor's computer can read without difficulty, and the two different formats, yours and hers, will have to be compatible. When you receive a set of galleys that are so messed up, that it takes you as long to review them as it took to write the book, it is past time to upgrade your word processor program to a newer version.

Aha. . . now it's time for the gravy. After you have sold your first serial rights, you can still sell the same work again, and again. There are rules of course, and these rules are regulated by the rights you have sold to the publication, and you must follow them. To sell the same information again the easiest method is to simply change the slant of the material being offered.

Suppose you wrote a piece and it was published in a nearby travel magazine. Say the piece provided instructions for making mud pies in the state of Washington. Then you found another market where you could submit the same manuscript, but this publication is located in Arizona. So you rewrite the article to indicate they'll need to add water to their dirt to make mud pies. You see, it's the same article, but with a different slant. Okay, this is a little too simple, but you get the idea.

Of course you can sell any manuscript completely unchanged as a reprint. These are known as second rights. You must remember which rights you have sold for your work as you go along, because some publications buy those rights for a year or more. You should also be aware that reprints do not sell for the same amount as a fresh manuscript might, the market is often half of the original price.

As an example, I once wrote a short magazine article, which took me about forty minutes to write.

I originally sold it for seventy-five dollars. Then I rewrote the article by changing the location information, and some text for a different line of thought, and sold it this time for an even one hundred dollars. I changed the text again for another location, and sold it this time for eighty-five dollars. Finally I sold it as a reprint for fifty dollars. Now think about this, I worked on that piece for forty minutes the first time, plus about five minutes two more times. I made three hundred and ten dollars for fifty minutes work, and I'm not through with it yet, as there is the international market to consider.

A trick you might want to consider is in sending your work to publications that do not overlap distribution areas. That is, sending it to publications where their readers are not likely to have read your work in another publication. This could be a place in the northern part of the United States, one in the south, one on the west coast, one on the east coast, and perhaps one or two in the central states.

You may want to deliberately refrain from selling some work to large international magazines, because it might be possible to make more money off the article by selling it to smaller magazines that don't overlap distribution areas.

If your work is published in large international magazines, odds are you're only going to sell the work once as First Serial rights, after that it's going to be Second rights.

GENRE'S
When you ask a new writer what they like to write about, or what kind of writing they like to do, the answer is rarely directly to the point. Instead of saying they want to write Children's books, perhaps Mysteries, or Historical, Science Fiction, even Romance novels, the wan'na be writer will say, "Fiction."

In the mind of a new writer, the word fiction covers just about anything that writer is interested in getting published no matter what it is. Most new writers do not have any idea of the varieties of Genre's that fit into the realm of 'Fiction.'

New writers must decide specifically what paths they want to travel in their quest for writing. Armed with this information they can help keep their direction on track, and traveling the best possible avenue.

WHAT IS THE BEST AGE FOR WRITING?
In a sense, there may not be a 'best' age for writers. There are however, good times to start writing, and good times to become published. The following information comes from research done by this author, and are based upon natural life cycles. As human beings, there are many cycles we go through in life. Those listed here, pertain to writers

The first potential time to begin writing is around the age of six or seven. Of course, if you think about your earlier years in school, you had the opportunity to learn this valuable skill. Those with a potential interest in writing can actually start from this point. This early age, is an age for many new forms of communicating with others. New languages are learned now, undoubtedly a few new words are learned that mothers hate to hear spoken. A whole world begins to open for the child, and writing is one of those skills acquired.

The next age bracket is twelve to fourteen, as children begin to find their place in the community, they find writing is required in many forms. Early thank you notes can bring out some inventive, and often poetic verse.

Followed by nineteen to twenty-one years of age. Writing skills are more important now in the work place, and this is an age that presents a potential opportunity in getting your first work published.

This can be an important age group, as the desire to write may start to arise during these years.

Twenty-six to twenty-eight are years where poetry can begin to flourish from the soul within, as some heavy lessons in life occur about this time. Poetry can be a form of releasing the burdens of life at this time, but the ability to write good prose will continue to grow within. As it happens, those who write poetry are often found to be the best writers of dialog as well.

Thirty-three to thirty five, can be busy years of writing. The long term writer often comes into play now. Just as often, as this age bracket begins to write, they may not recognize their own inner yearning for a writing career. They may write down lots of ideas about things they care about, such as Journaling. Or their writing can be in the form of helping others learn how to do certain job functions as in how-to-functions that they need to know to perform their work properly.

If a writer gets sidetracked into the "How-to" realm, and this happens, it could be the case because they never had the desire to write with the intention of being published, but they'll have another chance later in life.

Thirty-nine to forty-two, often this writing period may be primarily for the work place rather than for one's self. This is the age where someone may write company related materials, such as instruction booklets for products, or perhaps staff assigned columns for any number of publications. You most often see this writer's work listed as a publication column without a byline.

For those who have been writing steadily, forty-nine years of age to fifty-one, is a very good time for the opportunity to become part of the published community. Of course this won't take place if you haven't been writing before this point in time.

This can be a trying time in one's professional life. This is a time where most careers reach their early peak, and a time where some people decide that perhaps they have been following the wrong path in life. This condition brings about a few drastic changes in life styles. A time where those who have desired a writing career, make the change from the corporate life, to the private writing life, and the personal transition can be difficult.

Fifty-four, to fifty-six years of age is another time the hidden poet can come to life. Now however, the writing contains more depth and with more intense meanings, and with insights never before understood. This is also a time for other readers to understand the poets work when it is read. This is the age where the art form of poetry can really come to life.

Sixty to sixty-three is probably the best age for writers to emerge. Often this is the writer who didn't evolve in their early, or middle thirties. By now this writer has experienced life to the extent that they can truly portray its meaning on the written page.

As a younger writer these experiences cannot be imagined, they must be lived. Also, this is an age where retirement from the working world offers more time to the endeavors of writing. A time where a wan'na be writer can devote endless hours to the craft of writing, a direction many have desired for years.

Seventy-four to seventy-seven, most likely the last good chance at getting your work published. If you haven't written your memoirs yet, and you want to, do it before you're eighty-four. At the age of eighty-four, you may choose a whole new direction in life.

The best opportunity for writers, to start their publishing careers, but not the only times, are the ages of thirty-three to thirty-five, forty-nine to fifty-one, sixty to sixty-three.

PEN NAMES.
As a rule there is no need for Pen names this day in age, yet if you feel the need, one of those reasons could be to get work published that is outside your normal writing realm, perhaps a different Genre. This is a controversial topic. Some writers are against it, others swear by the use of pseudonyms.

There was a time when many women writers used pen names to get their work published. They did this because it was a man's world in many ways and being a writer was one of those ways. Men used them as well, but for different reasons.

There may be two situations arise that a pen name can come into use for today's writer. If you write for a publication that you do not want others to see your name used as a byline. Such as an 'Erotic' publication, or perhaps you are writing about something that could endanger your life. You should remember, anything of a legal nature could still come back to haunt you.

Using a pen name these days can lead to problems as far as taxes are concerned, and perhaps a few other monetary things. Or, if writing commercially, and explaining to an editor why he hasn't heard of you before. It's because you didn't use your real name, and why wouldn't you want the personal glory?

If you decide to write something using a 'Pen name,' the normal way to send your work would be as follows.

John Jones
1616 Nowhere St.
Somewhere USA
Phone me at 555-0000
E-mail me @ Pseudonym

'THE DAY I GOT LUCKY.'
By
Beau Line

It was a dark and stormy night, when I happened to see. . .

CO-WRITING.

Working with someone else as a co-writer on a book can become a huge problem when it comes to money. It may seem like a good idea in the beginning but it can become a headache in the long run. You can run into tax problems, or royalty division between the two of you, and this is when you are getting along. If one partner dies, who gets the proceeds, you, or the other writer's heirs? The best thing to do is just do all of your writing alone. The amount of situations that can arise are nearly endless.

Okay, a writing experiment can be of interest when Co-writing. If you want to learn how the opposite sex thinks, then you might get together with someone you trust, and co-author some stories between the two of you. It need not be anything you intend publishing, just to learn how the other side thinks and writes. It's eye opening, and it can be very entertaining for the both of you.

SASE's

Most writers are pretty savvy these days, at least the ones who are in contact with other writers or belong to a writer's group. Most writers understand they are required to send a Self Addressed Stamped Envelope, or SASE, with any correspondence to any editor.

You must remember editors often get hundreds if not thousands of pieces of mail weekly, or monthly. So if some unwary writer sends a manuscript to the editorial staff without an SASE, how far do you think it is going to get? Consider this, you sent some work into a publication and to the editorial staff you are an unknown source, immediately your envelope goes onto the larger slush pile to be read at some later date.

Finally an assistant editor gets around to reading through this slush pile. Your envelope gets sliced open, a hand reaches in and pulls out the top sheet, reads your query letter, likes it, and puts your work on top of the potential slush pile. This is the pile the actual story editor will read through when there is time to do so, usually the second week of the month.

The editor finally gets a few hours time, so the office door is closed, and the reading of the slush pile begins.

This slush pile has already been looked over by an assistant editor, so the editor who makes the final decisions knows this stack of mail may hold some promising work for the upcoming months ahead.

Your envelope is opened, the query letter is pulled out of the envelope, the editor quickly looks it over, likes the idea so he will drop you a note.

He looks for the SASE, and doesn't find one. He sighs with a slight moan, and places your query, back in the envelope from whence it came, perhaps back on the other pile behind him. Or, he may simply round file it. He would have sent you a note had there only been a SASE, too bad.

Sending an SASE nearly always guarantees an answer of some kind from an editor. To omit this courtesy, is costly. Professionals always send an SASE, and if one is not found with your query letter, it advertises the fact you are an amateur.

Even when you become well published, you still send an SASE.

Then there is a pile, or box full of material, which would normally be sent back to the writers if they have included postage. Or, the another pile of manuscripts, which will receive some kind of answer or form letter with squares checked off relating to the reasons the work cannot be used.

Titles are one way to hook the editor. Consider these two short opening paragraphs.

It's four O'clock in the morning at the hospital, and you awake to a startling sound. It's the curtains being brushed to one side near your bed, but you swear it's the soft flutter of her wings as she approaches your bedside. She is here for your blood, you shudder, and your blood veins tighten. You know her name, but in your mind you refer to her as the "Vampire."

She hovers quietly, her needle at the ready, and then she says those soft words she has practiced in the dark of the early morning hours, day after day. "Good morning Mr. Fountain. I'm sorry to wake you, but I have to draw a blood sample for your morning lab work."

Okay, now what do you use for a title? It has to be less than five words, but what? How about "Blood Suckers." Nope, to dramatic, too drastic, actually that title is almost offensive. Aha, 'ROOMING AT THE HOSPITAL.' Why, simply because no one actually rooms at a hospital, they are there because they have to be there.

If you title the article "Blood suckers," will it arouse the editor, maybe. Yet, "Rooming at the hospital," is a softer title, and will work better.

You must remember, when you send a manuscript to an editor, that editor may choose an entirely different title. A good working title helps in getting the point across to the editor quickly. If you can hook the editor, the editor knows you can hook the reader.

WRITER'S RIGHTS

FIRST SERIAL RIGHTS
These rights are offered to the magazine, or
newspaper, to publish your work for the first time.
If you send a manuscript to an editor, it is
understood that you are offering the right to
publish the work. It is up to you, the author, to
stipulate which rights are being offered. Most
book contracts will specify that the publisher has
first options on reprinting the book again, if sales
have proven worthwhile.

ONE TIME RIGHTS
A magazine (periodical) buys the right to publish
your work once. The geographical area is
generally that of the publications distribution area.

SECOND RIGHTS
Permits any other magazine the opportunity to
publish your work after it has been published
elsewhere for the first time. Second rights can be
sold several times, but, as a rule, do not pay as
much as the first serial rights.

ALL RIGHTS
This means exactly that. If you sell all your rights
to a piece, it is theirs forever. The publisher can
pretty much do what they want with the work in its
original form. All rights are not necessarily as
restrictive as you may think. The idea still belongs
to the writer. Sometimes you can get these rights

back from the publisher, but don't hold your breath. You can, however, rewrite the piece using the same information but written in a different manner, or with a different slant to the story. It can then be marketed for first rights. An all rights contract often pays more than any other rights for sale, but once you have sold all rights, that publication can use the same work again without paying the author more money for the work.

SUBSIDIARY RIGHTS.
These cover movies, television, radio, audiotapes, and translation rights.

TELEVISION, and MOVIE RIGHTS
These pretty well speak for themselves. These rights are Sold with the understanding that the work is to used in the entertainment field. Often a one year option is sold for these rights.

COPYRIGHTS
The copyright law unequivocally recognizes you, the writer, as the original owner. It grants you the privileges, and benefits that come with that ownership. It belongs to you the moment you finish writing it, no matter what it contains. Magazine articles, novels, short stories, whatever. Most often, anything you write is yours for life, plus fifty years. Do you want to put the copyright symbol ©, the date, and your name on each piece you send to an editor? You can, but it may just irritate the editor, and why would you want to irritate your editor? The editor already knows the

work belongs to you, that's why you are offered a contract of sorts for the right to use your work.

If you want to insure that your copyright is not infringed upon, consider registering your copyright. You may question, can I register all of my work with the copyright office? The answer is, "Of course you can." Yet you need to understand that currently it requires a monetary fee, filling out a TX form for each work, and time for the work to flow through the system. Is it worth it, not in this author's opinion, but only the writer can make this determination.

Should you encounter a Publisher who wants a "Copyright release." Which can transfer all of your rights to the publisher, often without compensation. You can change the wording of the RELEASE (by hand or?) Offer instead the right to publish and reprint your work for any purpose. What this amounts to, is you're letting them use your work. It's like renting your work out to the publication.

Though you own the copyright the moment the work is written, to protect it from infringement, you must register the copyright.

Titles, methods, ideas, procedures, slogans, and facts cannot be copyrighted.

You can obtain more copyright information from the "Copyright Office, Library of Congress,

Washington DC 20559 You can also obtain a TX form from them, and this form with a check for the currently required amount will get you a registered copyright on your work. Should you get this form, and decide to make a copy and send the copy, be sure the copy is perfect. It cannot eliminate any part of the wording, anywhere, to include the title, or headers or footers. To do so, will bring you an automatic rejection, and a delay in your registration.

Copyright registration for freelance writers.
http://www.asja.org/cwpage.htm.
You can download the copyrights forms from the Internet as an Adobe PDF file.
lcweb.loc.gov/copyright

WORLD or INTERNATIONAL RIGHTS.
Some magazines that are published in foreign countries also require these rights from the author before publication, and a foreign country is any country outside your own continental boundaries. Another point you must remember is even though your work is copyrighted by law in the United States, this right is not always observed worldwide. If the country in question is not a signed member of the "Berne Convention," your copyright may not mean a thing. The Berne convention is an agreement to protect the literary and artistic works.

ELECTRONIC RIGHTS.
These cover a wide range of media, from online magazines, CD-ROMs, or any method of transmitting the work electronically.

Electronic Rights are becoming more of an issue today than in the past few years. The laws since September 1999 are as follows.

Unless someone specifically transfers their ownership in writing, a non-employee writer owns the copyrights to their work exclusively.

Unless a specific written agreement exists, a publisher buys only the right to publish the freelanced work in one issue.

To include previous work in a database cannot be done without the author's permission.

You might express that the use is prohibited for online publication, or in electronic databases. This doesn't have to be a formal contract, it can be a written communication or your unchallenged notation in the upper right hand corner. "First Paper bound serial rights only."

The rights listed here, is a general description of what a writer has coming to them under most situations. Writer's rights are often confusing. In group discussions among writers, you will hear several definitions of the same topic.

The topic can be any one of the rights a writer owns in the beginning.

If you get to the point where you are seriously concerned about one of your rights as a writer, perhaps it is best if you contact a lawyer who handles this type of legality.

I have heard of an old method of proving your copyright. It is titled "Poor man's copyright." The method is to send yourself a copy of the work in the mail. The unopened envelope with its postmarked date is your proof of when you wrote the work inside. I cannot tell you this is foolproof, or if it will stand up in a court of law. Only that it has been used for decades.

PUBLIC DOMAIN.
Public domain work can be confusing. For work
that was published before January first nineteen
seventy-eight, or unpublished but registered, it
usually takes ninety five years after the work is
registered, for it to fall into the public domain.

However, if it was registered between January
first nineteen fifty, and December thirty first of
nineteen sixty-three, the author has to have filed a
renewal application within twenty eight years, or
the work becomes public domain.

For works created before January first nineteen
seventy-eight, and unpublished or unregistered as
of that date, that work belongs to the author's life
plus seventy years.

For works created after January first nineteen
seventy-eight, the copyright belongs to the author
for life, plus seventy years. For work owned
jointly, the copyright lasts for seventy years after
the last survivor.

For works made for hire, anonymous or
pseudonymous, the copyright lasts for ninety-five
years from the first publication, or one hundred
twenty years from creation, or whichever is
shorter.

AVERAGE DAILY MINUTES SPENT READING
BY AGE BRACKETS.

Age	1990 - 2000
Under 25	24
25 – 29	24
30 – 34	28
35 – 39	31
40 – 44	35
45 – 49	41
50 – 54	44
55 – 64	53
65 – 75	60
75 – 85	120 - 240

DEALING WITH EDITORS

You definitely want to be on the good side of this
person. Start your relationship with each editor
slowly, and professionally. Don't get personal with
an editor until you're established with the
publication, and then you should develop a good
rapport with the editor, and the publisher.

There will come a time, when an editor you've
been working with, leaves the publication. This
can be a tough situation if you have only been
dealing with the editor and not the publisher as
well. When this happens, you must start your
relationship over with the new editor. Now you
have to convince this new replacement editor that
your work is good, and that the publication needs
to keep you in its freelance writers Que.

It is not unusual for a publication to change its
direction slightly when a new editor comes
aboard, as editors are not always of the same
opinion. The changes come about because
publishers rely on their editors to select the proper
material for the publication, and often a new editor
can come up with new thoughts that the publisher
had not considered before.

Sometimes this is good, sometimes it's not. If it is
a very noticeable change, the readers will quickly
decide whether they like it or not, and the
publisher may again make a change.

Most publishers take a new editor under their wings to teach them how they want things done. This position is called an "Editorial assistant."

I recommend, if it is possible, you should keep in touch with any editors you get to know on a personal basis. If the editor moves to a new publication that can use your work, you may have an automatic market you hadn't counted on. If the editor doesn't move to another publication right away, send a personal note to his or her home, or E-mail address occasionally. It note doesn't have to be about anything special, just personal.

When you make preparations to send a hard copy of your work to an editor, that same editor may ask for a copy of the work on a computer diskette, or, perhaps as an attachment to an e-mail. When this request takes place, and this is not an unusual request these days, you must know what computer word processing format the editor uses, or what format she will expect from you that is compatible with her system. You can include a note in your query letter what computer word processing program you use, and what formats you can save your material in.

ASCII was at one time the most widely accepted, but some editors will insist on a particular format, such as .RTF, or Rich Text Format, .DOC, which stands for a Document file, and is used by Microsoft Word, or it could be .txt, which stands for a text file, and WPD which is a WordPerfect

Document. You need to find out what the editor prefers, and do it his way. Always keep a backup copy of your work, either a printed copy, or one on a diskette.

One important point about editors, You need them, at the same time they need you. An editor must maintain a stable of writers of which she can depend on for reliable work. If an editor loses a favored writer regardless the reason, it may be your break into the publishing world.

If an editor turns down your first work, don't try to figure out what is wrong with the editor, look instead at the work you sent to that publication. Most often this is where the problems are to be found. Read it again, and don't confuse your ability to write the piece, with a quality product. As a general rule, the problems arise when the piece is poorly written, or has been sent to the wrong kind of market.

A note of interest here. If you are dyslexic, but want to write, do so. As it happens a dyslexic writer produces work that comes across as different somehow. Editors may not be able to quite put their finger on what is different. Like a different kind of writers voice, but they like it and will use it to see if their readers like it as well.

Once editors become aware of you, they can tell your work without seeing your name on the written page. This is your writer's voice, and this is what editors purchase. Your work must be good of course, but it is the way you present it that attracts an editor into using your material. Take care when you send your first work to an editor. If you send a mediocre manuscript, this is what the editor will expect each time, or he will expect it to be worse.

As a new writer you need to think about what kind of paper you use in your printer, and your typewriter. Especially when you send it to an editor of your choosing. You may think your paper is fancy, or perhaps you just like the color of the paper, but as a rule editors don't like these fancy colored manuscripts. Editors like white, twenty-pound, letter size paper, with easy to read letter quality print, on one side only.

When you finish the work, think about what size envelope should you use to mail your work to the editor? If it is only going to include a page or two, the smaller six inch by nine inch envelope will work satisfactorily. A few writers send short manuscripts folded three times and stuffed into a number ten envelope.

Most editors prefer the work not be folded more than once. A flat, clean manuscript is appreciated, because it doesn't bend up toward them while they are reading it. With this in mind, the cost of a larger nine inch, by twelve inch envelope is not that much more expensive. I'd suggest any manila envelope that will accept the completed work without folding.

For larger works, the Post Office has a great, and fairly inexpensive box you can purchase for larger manuscripts.

You should already know this, but for the less informed writer, you must double space any manuscript you send to an editor. The editor uses the space between lines to make notes. These are notes the editor deems necessary for changes in the work. Margins are to be one inch on each side, with your name and address on the top of the first page, and a header on the following pages containing the title, your name, and page number.

Editors are very busy people. Do them, and yourself, a favor. Do not leave what is called a 'Widow,' at the top of a page. A widow is a single line of type, which is the last line of a previous page. Publishers hate them. Invariably a typesetter misses them, and then the story line that follows makes little, if any sense. An 'Orphan' is a single line of text left at the bottom of the page, and is the first line of work from the following page.

You might want to consider placing the word "END" or –30- or #### just a few lines down from the end of your story line. These notations tell the typesetter, or editor, that this is the end of the work. Of course, you'd think they'd know that.

Once you become a published writer, it is a good practice to send an occasional, "Thank you." note to the editor using your work. It reinforces their opinion of having made the correct choice to use your work in the beginning. Also, the editor, like anyone else, enjoys knowing you appreciate them.

Another useful note about sending your work to editors. On the outside of your manila envelope, print very clearly the editor's name in the lower left-hand corner. If you choose, you can also write it in large letters on the back of the envelope. Both methods assure that the correct editor gets the manuscript as quickly as possible. If not it can miss a day or two getting from the incoming mail desk, to your chosen editor's desk.

It's rare, but it happens, a publication goes out of print, and it may owe you money for work previously published. You might get paid, you might not. Be polite, send an invoice once a month, and hope for the best. It will do little good to get angry with the editor, as it's out of the editor's hands, and remember this is also an editor who is out of a job. If it's a great deal of money owed you, you can contact an Attorney. If it's less than two or three hundred dollars and you hire an Attorney to collect it, guess who's going to end up with most of the money. It won't be you.

Read any publication guidelines, and you will see that nearly all of them ask for a query letter, or a cover letter. Perhaps a query letter with a synopsis, or even the first ten pages, or first three chapters.

If possible, drop by the publication that uses your work to meet, and speak with any editor you are working with. Be sure you contact the editor ahead of time, mentioning your intent. The best time to do this can vary from one publication to the next, but normally the better time would be about the second week of the month.

The last week is their deadline, and the first week is production, neither is a time an editor want to be sitting around talking with anyone not involved in getting the publication into print and out on the street.

Then there is the time that you may be away on vacation, or a period of time you will be unavailable to any editor. If there are editors you work with on a regular basis, it might be a good idea to send a note to those editors letting them know when you will be gone and when you expect to return.

WILL EDITORS OR PUBLISHERS STEAL YOUR WORK?

It probably has happened, but normally editors wouldn't take that chance, nor do they think that way. However, you must remember that you are not the only writer in the world who uses their mind to come up with new ideas. So, when an editor says, "We currently have a similar piece in place." Accept it for the truth, and move along.

SAMPLE LETTERS

Anytime you are conferring with an editor about a manuscript, consider sending a list of sample items you can provide for the same editor of the publication you are working with.

SAMPLES LIST

A samples list should not be sent to an editor in your original query letter. Once you are established with an editor, you can send a list of other work you feel may be of interest to that editor, and that publication.

SAMPLES
List of boat modification projects.
First rights are available on these articles.

'SEA WATER STRAINERS.'
658 words, 1 drawing
Most boaters' feel any marine engine water-cooling system needs to be filtered regardless the geographical area a boat is moored in. Yet, surprisingly many boats come off a production line without sea water filters of any kind. Having encountered this problem I began checking into sea water strainers, and yes there were obstacles. I couldn't find one within a reasonable price range, or the ones offered were much larger than my small four-cylinder engine needed. Also, finding room for a larger filter in my engine compartment presented a problem. Then I came across an easy, simple cure.

'ADJUSTING YOUR COMPASS.'
536 words 1 drwg
It's dark, and you look at your illuminated compass heading, yes it says you are on course, but is it really the correct compass course you want? Not necessarily, the numbers may be the right digits, but is your compass accurate. With a little effort on your part, it could be closer to what you expect, and afford you a more comfort in any heading you choose to follow.

Second rights are available to the items listed below.

CAREENING IS FAST AND EASY.'
976 words Two drwgs.
Often a condition comes up that requires your attention to some detail under the boat, perhaps a knot meter that is no longer working, a propeller that needs to be changed, a gouge in the hull that needs to be patched. Yet you don't want to haul the boat out at the time. The easiest solution is to do like the sailors of old. Careen the boat. It's easy, fast, and cheap.

PRACTICE CELESTIAL NAVIGATION ANYWHERE.' 717 words 1 drwg
My celestial navigational skills just go out the window if I can't practice them and a false horizon mirror just never quite did the trick for me. I'm like most of you, I just don't seem to find myself offshore much either. Of course if I got out there I'd have to work hard at finding my longitude and latitude, because I'm out of practice.

On a recent day while out sailing I happened to look over the stern of the boat, at the horizon to the south. Lo and behold I realized I actually had a horizon. I thought about my need to practice my celestial navigation, and now I knew how to practice It anytime I wanted.

SAMPLE DEMAND LETTER
Writer's Markets Jan. 2000

Dear (Editor or publisher's name):

I have been in touch with (name of person with whom you've been dealing) on (the date in question) in regards to my request for payment of the article / short story / poem (insert title) Published in the (publication date) issue of (publication name). I still have not received any response from your offices.

I respectfully request that I be paid for the following:

• Article (name of article, issue date and amount promised)

• Any other expenses / promised payment (includes expenses,

Postage, phone calls – anything you spent trying to get paid.

• Late payment fee $100.00

• TOTAL AMOUNT DUE: $ -----

I have included copies of the above, as well as pertinent E-mails, and correspondence. I sincerely hope this matter will be taken care of as soon as possible.

If the above amount is not received within fifteen (15) working days, I will be forced to pursue other action (list here what you may do: Go to your writer's organizations, union, small claims court, Better business Bureau, and /or a lawyer.

Thanking you in advance,

AB Writer.

BY LINES

Will you get a byline for your writing? You should. While looking at a publication you're interested in submitting work to, you will see some items listed in the table of contents have bylines, and some don't. The articles listed that have bylines are freelanced, or produced by regular contributing writers, which is about the same thing. A regular contributing writer is a freelance writer who has become well established with the publication.

The articles, columns, or departments without bylines are staff written, thus off limits to you as a freelance writer. Basically staff writers are 'For fee writers.' That is, they're paid to produce the work, and the work does not belong to them, nor does the copyright. Their work and the copyright belong to the publication.

On occasion you will see a regular column with a byline, but this is a position of respect given to the writer by the publication. Once a writer becomes well known, and their column is well read, they can insist on, and get a byllne. When you see a byline name on a column, or a department, check the list on the publication's mast head. Often you will see that same name, as one of the staff members.

When you find a publication you are interested in writing for, read the editors letter, and letters to the editor. Reading the editors letter will give you an idea where his interests lie, and when you read the letters to the editor, you will find what the readers think, and want from the publication.

Either place gives you an idea of what you can contribute, and what the editor may snap up for an upcoming edition.

SENDING UNSOLICITED MATERIAL

When you decide to send unsolicited material, the first thing you need to do is to find out if the publication will accept unsolicited material. If you have a copy of the publication's writer's guidelines, read them thoroughly. Somewhere they will tell you if the editor requires a query letter first. If this is the case, the guidelines may also tell you that all unsolicited manuscripts will not be read? If you do not heed these directions, you are dooming your work before you get your foot in the editor's doorway. If, in reading the guidelines, it is not spelled out, feel free to send your work as an unsolicited manuscript.

If the publication does accept unsolicited manuscripts, several things can happen. First, as an unknown source, your work will go into the "Unknown writers," slush pile. Yes, the high one on the table against the wall, and if the pile is actually stacked, that will be very unusual. In some cases it will be boxes of envelopes containing manuscripts. Perhaps your manuscript will get read shortly after its arrival. Perhaps it won't get read for some time.

Second, after you do become known to the publication as a reliable writing source, your work will go into the preferred slush pile. This slush pile is closer to the editor's desk, perhaps even within reach.

Third, as often happens, an editor can find herself with an unexpected slot to fill in the upcoming issue. This often happens just prior to publishing the current issue. Where does the editor go for a filler article? That's correct, to the preferred slush pile. If she can't find anything there that she likes, she will go to the slush file of unknown writers. She will be seeking something that can be used for the slot that is presently open. Is this your break? It can be if it interests the editor. Catch her attention when you can, because you may only get one shot at this publication.

Here is where a new writer gets lucky. It is easier for an editor to use something she has in house, than to answer a query letter, and then having to wait for a questionable manuscript. If her deadline is close she is not going to wait, she needs it now.

As a writer, often just looking at the front cover of a magazine will tell you what's hot at the time. You also need to look inside the magazine and read the editor's monthly letter. The editor's letter will tell you what she is interested in seeing from her writers, though it doesn't actually say this.

The savvy writer will try to send the editor something pertaining to her editorial letters. While you're looking at the magazine, look at the table of contents, articles with bylines, are usually written by freelance writers. Staff written articles rarely have bylines, and are generally monthly columns. These are not open to freelance writers.

If you send a suggestion to one of the column writers, it will not get used.

It is not an unusual occurrence for an editor to send personal notes to favored contributing writers, sometimes apologizing for not getting back to the writer sooner about some manuscript the editor is interested in, but has been holding for a particular publication issue.

As an author, if you feel the need, you can write, "Exclusive to your circulation area," in the upper right hand corner of your query letter, or your cover letter. Then on the first page of the manuscript, in the upper left corner, put the copyright symbol, your name, and "One time rights." You might do this if you plan on sending the manuscript to more than one publication, at a time, and a publication's whose circulation areas do not overlap one another.

You should keep in mind that once you have written something it is legally copyrighted. You know this and so does the editor. So, placing a symbol of copyright on your work is a waste of time.

A TRICK YOU CAN USE FOR ATTENTION

As a writer you want your manuscript to be read as soon as possible when it is received by the editorial offices of your choosing. Odds are it won't get looked at any sooner than any other writer's work unless you can entice the editor, or assistant editor to read yours before the others.

The trick then is to draw attention to your envelope. You can do this by using a wide tip color marker pen to draw a line along all the edges of your manila envelope. Use a color that catches the eye, perhaps a color that is pleasing but not garish. Of course the color is your decision. Once you choose a color, use the same color consistently on all the envelopes you send to your editors.

When an editor begins to use your work, and she finds herself in need of a quick story line, she'll look for an envelope with the green line around the edges. Once you have established a good reputation in the editorial office, it won't matter which slush pile your manuscript is in, or where your work is in that pile. With the line around the edge, and being known to the editor, it is the same as being on top of the pile on her desk.

However, if you mark your envelop in this manner and the work is not up to standards, it will still get discarded. The problem arises the next time you send something to this same editor. When the line around the edges shows up, it may automatically get tossed out.

REJECTION LETTERS

According to everything you hear, rejection slips, or letters, are not a good thing to receive, or are they? When you receive a rejection letter from a publisher, read it carefully, and read between the lines. Why was your work rejected? Did the editor spell it out for you?

This is a file of letters writers do not want to accumulate, and few will acknowledge that they even have these letters. Yet this is a file folder every writer will have in their desk or a box somewhere near their writing area. If a writer does not have an editor's rejection letter file somewhere, they are not writing. That, or the writer has thrown the letters into the trash. It is nearly impossible for a writer to send a copy of their manuscript to the proper editor, or correct publication every time. Hence, rejection letters.

There are different kinds of rejection letters. Form letters that say little, and only have boxes with check marks made in one of two places. Maybe a personal note attached to your original query letter, and returned inside your SASE, or a form letter that has an added note from the editor. The publications letter head with a short note of encouragement from the editor.

Letters that say the publication does not accept the particular rights you offered on your last manuscript offered to them. Letters explaining the publication is not accepting any material for another two years, which can be a lifetime to the writer. Letters indicating your work does not meet their current editorial needs, and the list of rejection letter reasons seems to be endless.

If you are a writer who has been throwing these letters away, stop doing so, you need to keep these in a file somewhere. You keep these because they are of value to you. Oh yes, but they are valuable. Rejection letters are clues to your writing abilities, and to your marketing skills. Examine each letter, and think about its contents in regard to the work you sent to this publication.

If the editor told you the material was too short, offer to rewrite it to suit his needs. Articles are harder to shorten than to lengthen. If it's too long, then of course you have to offer to shorten the piece. Perhaps you can offer the additional information you have gathered as a side bar.

Did you choose the wrong publication? If so, do your homework more thoroughly and send it to the proper publication next time. Often an editor's personal note will spell out the problems as to why your work was incorrect. If this is the case, make the correction before you submit the work again. If it is a matter of publishing rights, perhaps you can approach the same editor with another offer to include the rights the publication needs in order for them to accept your manuscript.

If it is a situation involving a lengthy span of time before the publication is open to more manuscripts, don't wait, send your manuscript to another publication.

Not only do book publishers run into this situation, but even magazines can have a two year lull in accepting any new work. This causes problems for both parties, the writer cannot wait for the publisher to begin accepting work again, and the publisher often loses potentially good writers for the same reason.

On occasion, a perfectly good manuscript will not be accepted just because it didn't catch the editor's eye right off the bat. This could be the leading paragraph didn't grab her attention, or simply the title didn't sound interesting. Sometimes a simple change of title will do the trick, or just rewriting the lead in paragraph, could help make a sale.

Whatever you do be polite and professional in dealing with the editor. If the piece is completely wrong, then of course you are out of luck.

When you confront an editor about a rejected manuscript, you better know the publication very well so you can make your point in the proper manner.

Once you have all of your suggestions figured out, the changes you are willing to make, and why you feel this piece is correct for the publication that has sent you the rejection letter. You can try again.

WRITING & RESEARCH

When you first begin to write, research is not the key issue as writing will be the foremost thing in your mind. Yet it doesn't take long until you discover the need to do some research on what it is you want to market. This research can involve any number of items. It can be the correct spelling of a name, a part number for a "How – to" article. A travel location for back packers, high tides for a future coastal beach outing or anything related to your current work project.

The information you find as to your research should accompany your manuscript when you send it to a publisher. When this information accompanies the manuscript, you the writer, add a higher potential of selling your work to an editor. If you do the homework first it can open a door for you. Don't expect an editor to research your facts for you.

Writers for the most part, can research any medium they wish to write about. An author who pens a book telling a reader at home how to change spark plugs in any gasoline engine, doesn't have to understand various spark plug electrode gaps, or heat ranges for various engine performance. The author only needs to understand how to use various wrenches and sockets.

However, the author who wants to write specialized books, needs to fully understand a great many, and various conditions that will be encountered while doing their manuscript research. There is the chance that like most specialized fields, you can't write about them unless you are one of the specialists. Or, at the least, well schooled in the subject.

Do you need to be well aware of your chosen subject before you write about it? No, as a rule you don't have to, but you need to know how to do the research on your topics of interests. Some times you will be able to find a great amount of information on the Internet, but you also need the ability research your projects without the aid of computer programs. That's correct, the old fashioned hard way. Your local library is a great source of information.

Keep in mind that the Internet is still very young, and there are writers presenting information on the Internet that is erroneous in its content. They may offer information to the reading public, but are they qualified in the field they are writing about, or are they just using someone else's work. With this in mind, it might be best if you double check your work at the library that contains any information you gain from the Internet.

Surprisingly, over time you may find that after you have penned several books on a subject, that you are considered the expert that others look to for information.

Today, most larger publishers have a staff in place that do nothing but review the work authors have sent to them for consideration. If it passes a preliminary inspection, and is accepted for potential publication, the editor will go through a more thorough examination of the information that has been supplied.

In the second review, all the facts the writer has presented with the manuscript will be verified. If you the writer have done your homework, and the story line can be edited to fit the issue the publication has in mind, you may be offered a contract for the piece.

On the other hand, if you have not done your homework adequately, you may instead receive a simple rejection note with little if any information as to why your work has been rejected. Editors and publishers cannot afford to have erroneous information published in their publication. It's as simple as that.

Even then, research is not all that simple. You cannot copy the information from a book and use it in your work. Well you can but you must have permission to do so and you must give credit to the source of your information. Instead, you should read several books, learn all about your subject and make notes as you study, and then write what it is you feel is the truth of the matter.

If you do not have the knowledge, you can't pull the wool over the eyes of others for very long. To expect to produce something in writing for others to read when you lack the knowledge, professional or novice, you abilities will soon be discovered if ill informed.

QUERY LETTER REQUIREMENTS.

So, you've found a publication on the magazine rack at the supermarket, and it's one you think you can write an article for. You have an idea to submit to the magazine, and the story you have in mind will fit into the publication's needs. For whatever reason, you don't want to purchase the magazine at this moment, but you need to know the current editor's name, and how to contact the publication in regards to your idea.

You must always address your query letter to the current editor. At some point if you do write for this magazine it is a good idea to become a subscriber as well. Doing so allows you to keep up with the magazines publishing interests, and provides you with the monthly editor's letter to the readers.

Do this, look inside the magazine and within the first few pages you should find the publication's masthead which is the listings for the business staff, the magazines mailing address, and the names of the editorial staff. Find the editor's name, and look around the vicinity of the business address portion to see if they list an E-mail address as well. Write these down so that you will have them later, then before you put the magazine back onto the shelf, find the table of contents and look up the letter from the editor.

These may have a number of titles, but it is the letter from the editor to his reading public. This can be an open door for writers. In the editor's letter, it is explained what the editor's thoughts are at the time of this current publication. Send the editor something that fits into her current interests, and you will find yourself a receptive editor. Your query letter must also have the correct address of, and the spelling of the editor's name.

Another very good source for publications, and a current editor's list, is to look in the book. "Writer's Markets." You can also check with your local library, to see if they have a book titled 'R.R.BOWKER BOOKS IN PRINT.' They will also have these lists for magazines in print.

Non-fiction markets nearly always require a query letter, but fiction markets do not. Many fiction editors just want to see how well you write. These same editors may not bother with reading queries, but a cover letter should always accompany a fiction manuscript.

ONE PAGE ONLY.

You can break a few query letter rules, but there are some you must not break. If you do, the reasons better be good. Most editors require a one page query letter. Editors feel that if you cannot explain what your story idea is in one page, it is an indication that you may not fully understand the idea yourself. A one page query letter is almost a required qualification.

If you have enough room on your one page query letter, consider adding a one paragraph sample opening for the work you're presenting.

Though a one page query is essential, a cover letter can accompany your query letter on a second page, but cover letters are rarely required at this time.

Most publication's writers guidelines will tell you, that if you want anything returned, photographs, manuscript, anything at all, you must send the proper size envelope, and the correct postage to pay for its return, and of course a note making your wishes known in these respects.

When possible, include the market potential for the manuscript you are submitting in your query letter. Acquiring the marketing information for your kind of article may not be an easy task. Basically it would be those readers who might find interest in your work.

Let's say your article is along the lines of, "How to build a computer office into a hall closet." You might find markets with a Home office publication, Parenting magazines, or possibly some wood working magazines.

You should explain how this closet office will work, such as, a chair could be stored under the table top which containing the computer video monitor. Also that the table has a fold down leaf for a working surface, and that a trash can is stored under the chair, and the keyboard pulls out from under the table for use. The computer is stored against one wall, if it is a desktop tower style. Also when the door is fully opened another pull down shelf mounted on the back of the door is used for books or other paperwork while you are working. Of course it will crowd the hallway, but it will offer some degree of privacy to the user.

If you try marketing this same work to a parenting magazine you will have to explain why, and how a mother can take advantage of this small area for this kind of project. How and why it can save other needed space in an already crowded home for what the parent considers more required needs.

A book query's intention is to get the editor to ask you for a full book proposal, or the entire manuscript. There are times when a page and a half for a book query letter are accepted, but never more than two pages. Never.

The normal procedure for a non-fiction writer and new writers is to send a query letter to the publication, or publisher of their choice. Especially if the manuscript is lengthy, such as a textbook. Most short stories or articles can be sent without a query letter, but a cover letter must be included.

If an editor cannot tell from your query letter, how well you write, or about your writing ability, but he is interested in your proposal, he may ask for clips of your previous work. This tells you, the author, that you need to improve your Query letter writing skills next time. It seems that one sixth of all query letters earn their writers a chance at being published in the publication.

It is not uncommon for an editor to try new writers as often as possible. The editor does this with the understanding that at some point he will loose one or two of his present stable of regular writers.

When it comes to the use of personal letterhead stationary, some writers use it, most writers don't. If you elect to use letterhead stationary, do so on the first page only. Generally a fancy letterhead produced on high quality paper with lots of ornamental stuff, or scented, only impresses one person.

That person is the one who sends it out in the mail originally, not those who receive it on the other end of its travels. One exception to this line of thinking, may be the writer's resume.

Don't discuss fees in a query letter. If you mention a fee that is too high, it will kill your chance with this editor. If it is to low he'll think you don't know the value of your work. The editor will make you an offer If he likes your work, then you can decide either to accept it, or refuse it. Be realistic here, twenty minutes work is not worth hundreds of dollars.

Keeping copies of any correspondence, with any editor, or publication, regardless of the content, is always prudent. These copies will at some point in time serve you well, when dealing with an editor who may say, "Did I ask you for photographs, or line drawings?"

Perhaps a manuscript had been scheduled, but it doesn't appear in the edition you expected. Do you have a copy of the dates the editor said it would be published? If so you can refer to that letter, or E-mail note, and you will have the answer.

Sometimes no news is good news. If you don't get a rejection letter, it can mean the editor is holding your work for a later or more appropriate publication.

SLANTED TO THAT PUBLICATION.
The editor receives your proposal and it says.
"Dear editor. I'm offering one time North American
rights on the work I have included for your
consideration. If interested please call me at
1-800-777-7777." Signed, Becky Mulling it over.

Is this editor going to call Becky? Not much
chance of that happening. If your proposal is
general in appearance, the editor will think you
have not done your homework, and that you are
sending out multiple queries for the same piece of
work.

If you want to work with an editor, you better use
their name on the letter, and though you don't
know the editor personally, you can still express
some personal feelings.

Such as starting out with the correct publications
name at the top and putting the editor's name and
title in bold capitol letters.

Such as "WILLIAM DANIALS – EDITOR,"

Doing this shows respect, and it draws attention to
their name on the top of your letter. An editor is an
ordinary person just like the rest of us, and has
worked hard to get this position in life. Having paid
his or her dues, the editor is proud to be sitting in
this chair.

You might even consider putting the editor's name before the name and address of the publication.

When you start the main body of your letter you can start in a friendly manner such as, 'Good Morning William.' This is one way to start your letter that will be friendly and personal, but don't get gushy or over friendly. Above all else, be honest in your dealing with the editor.

Your letter to an editor will contain your name, address, phone number, E-mail address if you have one, and any titles or professional letters. Titles or letters, are credentials, such as a degree in the arts, communications field, or any subject you may be writing about. Even as simple as Mr. or Mrs. Also, let the editor know if you have photographs or line drawing available for the work you are offering.

In providing your writing qualifications to the editor, it provides the editor with confidence in your ability to write what you are proposing. Your qualifications are your personal experiences or knowledge of the subject matter. It is necessary for you to instill confidence that you are the one to write about the subject.

Don't try to fake this information with borderline truths. In the first place the editor has been in the business longer than most writers and can spot questionable information quickly. In the second place if you do fool the editor you can't fool yourself, and when it shows up on the printed page, everyone will know your real ability.

PUBLISHING BACKGROUND

You've heard it said that if you are not a published writer, don't say so in a query letter, and this is true. If you are published, you can offer clips of your previous work to an editor if it is in a similar or related field.

In case you are really new to the publishing world you should know that clips are copies of your work previously accepted in other publications. Editors may, or may not ask for them if you offer to send them clips. Simply making the offer may tell the editor what they want to know.

You may be surprised to learn that editors can often tell from the way you present yourself in your query letter, if you've been published before. It's kind of written between the lines, a second sense perhaps.

As a final note here, I've been writing for so long that I have file drawers full of copies of previous works published. I have never had a publisher as me for clips, but who knows, it could happen.

Your name and address

SAMPLE QUERY LETTER.
THE EDITOR'S NAME Publications Manager
AMERICAN FEDERATION of ASTROLOGERS
PO Box 22040
Tempe, AZ. 85285

Good Morning.
In a recent reading of the American Federation of
Astrologer's product price list, I found twenty-two
books offered on the subject of self-taught
astrology. There were more that hinted as to that
direction, but their titles did not address the issue
enough to know for certain. I'd like to fill a gap left
open to many astrologers. That is the teaching of
astrology. The book I'm currently working on,
"HOW TO TEACH ASTROLOGY" is well
underway and can be made available to you. I've
been teaching astrology since nineteen sixty-four,
about the same time I first joined the Federation.
This book will encompass many items the
Astrologer needs to know about to teach
beginning, or advanced classes, and what outline
they should consider for the classes they offer.
This includes class sizes, costs, what's provided,
what's needed, confidentiality, and personal
involvement.

Drop a line as to your interest when you can.
Thanks.

DB Author

SAMPLE QUERY LETTER.

Your name
Address
Somewhere USA
E-mail me @
April 8th, 1999

ELLYCE ROTHROCK Managing Editor
Sea Magazine
17782, Cowan
Irvine, CA. 92614

Good Morning.
The article I'm proposing is one about our granddaughter and her first time aboard our boat. A pleasure, but a different kind of learning experience for her grandfather.

My wife and I have been living, and cruising, onboard our sailboat, 'Itchy Feet,' for nine years. During this period of time we have had numerous guests, and relatives aboard. Some for overnight trips, but most were only aboard for a day's adventure.

None of these early excursions prepared us for having grandchildren aboard for summer trips. When we started taking them for lengthy trips, we derived great pleasure from their eye opening company, and everyone aboard learned new things.

As more boaters are in, or near, the retirement age, more grandchildren will be found aboard private boats. This article can save another grandparent some pleasurable anguish. Yes there is such a thing.

Ellyce, I'm published in fifteen magazines across the country, six of which are boating related. I can send clips if you desire, and I can submit photos for the article.

The article is written and can be in your hands within a few days. Please send me a note when time permits.

Thanks, I appreciate your time.
Author

THIS LETTER IS MORE A PITCH TO GET TO
KNOW A NEW EDITOR.

CAROL McDONALD – EDITOR
Heartland Boating
319 N. Fourth Street.
Suite 650St. Louis, MO. 63102

Good morning Carol
Carol, your title, according to my last letter from
Frank, is that of editorial assistant. Perhaps it's
presumptuous of me, but I feel if you're sitting in
the chair, you've got the job.

In response to the same letter, I'm sending a short
list of potential articles I'd like you to consider for
next year's publication schedule. Frank still has
one or two of this type article. Such as
"Anchoring." Perhaps "Comforts of living aboard."
I've another item or two I'll explain to you later
when I have them ironed out a little more.

Just to give you a little background on myself, I
write for eight or nine different magazines
ongoing. Mostly boating, but a few other interests
as well. This year you folks have been kind
enough to publish several of my do-it-yourself
informational articles. I thank you for that.

I'm curious, is there a burn out problem with editors, as there is in several occupations. I'm asking because Marsha is the second editor I've lost due to new avenues in life, and both editors within the past two years.

Carol, I wish you well in your new position, and anything I can do to make it easier, I'll certainly consider.

Thanks again.

Author

This letter resulted in a contract for ten articles, and several feature stories. Though of a personal nature, I had already established myself in writing abilities for the magazine the previous year.

The following is a sample of events that take place through the Internet E-mail, and took place before flash drives existed.

FROM   Author's E-mail address
TO   Publisher's E-mail address
DATE   April 1999
SUBJECT Book Proposal

Editor's Name.
When last we communicated, September of 1998, I mentioned a book I'd like to send for your consideration. You sent me your writer's guidelines, and I believe I have followed those ideas as requested.

This book's theme is do-it-yourself projects. Its present working title is "SIMPLE BOAT PROJECTS," and I am ready to send it to your designated address. Presently it is eighty-five pages, contains forty-two drawings, and the word count is thirty one thousand words.

I can send it on diskettes with the book saved in any program that is compatible with MS Word, or WordPerfect. The drawings can be sent on a diskette, but I will send a hard copy as well.

The above E-mail letters resulted in the following response.

FROM   Publisher's E-mail address
TO Author's E-mail address DATE   April 1999
SUBJECT Book Proposal

Author's name
I am happy to hear you have it completed and I would like to see a copy ASAP. I am certain if this is what we discussed, we would be very happy to publish the book, as we have no other similar title. If all goes well, it can be released by mid to late May.

Please mail it to the following address.

This book went on the market and did well. Due to a hurricane in Florida the publisher is now out of business and the books rights have been returned to me.

COVER LETTERS.
A cover letter is less crucial than your query letter, as a cover letter travels with your manuscript. Yet, it can play a part in the editor's decision to purchase your work. A cover letter should be brief, three paragraphs should do it.

It will introduce your work to the editor, and provide a sample of your manuscript's contents. How the story flows, and perhaps the writer's rights being offered. The cover letter may also offer sidebar material, and whether you expect to get the manuscript sent back to you. Some writers believe you shouldn't explain your story in a cover letter, others feel you should. I feel it is okay to send a brief note about the story line. If the editor likes the brief note, he will make you an offer. If not, the two of you have saved unnecessary time conversing over the subject.

A cover letter tells the editor whom you are, where you live, and how you can be reached. What the story is about, and if you are offering photo's, drawings, or illustrations that can be used.

You will find some writer's guidelines specify you should include your social security number on the front page of the manuscript you are offering for publication. I never provide mine until the editor and I have come to an agreement.

This is a personal thing with me, I just don't want my social security number out there floating around loosely. This is of course, your choice.

Don'ts.
Start out with "Dear sir, or Madam." This is too vague, and sends a message that you're sending it to everyone.

"I'm sending you a story you can't refuse."

"I need to sell you this article so I can buy shoes for my children."

"I can send this somewhere else if you don't want it."

"I don't cook much, but I found this recipe for fudge, that. . "

"Please pass this along to the editor who handles this kind of . . . ."

COVER LETTER SAMPLE.

The Author
625 Front St.
Somewhere USA

September 2011

The Current Editor
The Magazine of Fantasy and Science Fiction
PO Box 1806
Madison Square Station
New York, NY. 10159-1806

Good Morning.
The novelette I'm sending for your consideration is 15,900 words, and a science fiction story.

Samuel Chambers and Michele Stevens were trapped in a period of time where individuals who were found to be undesirable's, in their community, were eliminated from society.

Michele Stevens a woman of power, has come to the attention of the *"CENTRAL COMMITTEE."* Rumors have been circulating that she had in essence taken over some adjoining territory that was not under her jurisdictional control.

Samuel Chambers, an Investigator for the Central committee, has been assigned to investigate her. Should he find reason to suspect her as guilty of crimes against the community, he is to deliver her to The Committee. The central committee will in turn will review her standings in the community, and decide her fate. If she is found guilty she will be sent to the Eliminator. The Eliminator, a title of rank, will in turn would place her inside the Carbophylica Purification Chamber, where the particle beam defuser would eliminate her, and all public record of her would then be erased. One problem emerged between Samuel Chambers and Michele Stevens. Love, and survival.

If you cannot use this story line, please do not return it. Just destroy it, and drop me a note when time permits.

Thanks for your time.
Author

March 9, 2010

June Monday
SOMEONE PUBLISHING
PO Box 111111
Nice place, ON K9V 4R8 Canada

Good Morning June.
Since our last discussion Via the Internet e-mail,
I've rewritten the piece to include the newer circuit
board which has an off/on switch mounted on it as
well. Yet I've indicated to your readers that they
can build the board without the switch at their
choosing.

This is Thursday and I took photos this morning. I
expect to have them back in the morning, which
should put this in the mail to you by tomorrow
about lunch time.

June, I'm assuming that you will send me a
complimentary copy for my files. I sent you an IRC
coupon but I do not know if that will cover the cost
of sending the publication copy. If not please feel
free to deduct that expense from the check you're
sending for the article.

I want you to know that I appreciate your using my
work, and look forward to a long term relationship
between ourselves.

Thanks again for your time.
Author

INFORMATION PACKAGE.

The information you can send with each query letter, or cover letter, is of your own choosing, but you should consider the following items.

1. A personalized query letter.

2. Author's biography

3. The list of your publishing history.

4. Your list of qualifications, for writing the work you are currently presenting.

5. A list of your references, and resources for fact checking, and they will be checked.

6. Table of contents, if the work you're sending has a table of contents.

7. A synopsis.

8. Outline

NOTE:
Each attachment you send with your query letter, should be referred to in the query letter by page number, and title.

Synopsis length? Your choice, but keep it as short as possible.

BOOK PROPOSAL PACKAGE

Book proposal packages can differ from those of a manuscript package. They may differ in what the editor requires of the writer. Sometimes it is not spelled out as to which the editor wants, a synopsis, or an outline.

If it is chapter outlines, these need to be concise, and clear in what each chapter is about. Outlines can be lengthy, perhaps as many as thirty pages.

Chapters, when required by an editor, need to be consecutive. You cannot choose a chapter here, and a chapter there. They must be in consecutive order. Editors can tell from reading a chapter or two if they want to continue reading more.

TITLES & ENDINGS.
Titles and endings are often your keys to success.
They advertise your work and your ability. Choose
them carefully.

Titles are followed by a paragraph that grabs the
editor, and then the reader's attention. Titles can
be tricky, but once mastered, they will become
second nature to the writer. When you pick up a
book, or a magazine, what is the first thing you
look at? The titles of course, then the back page.

It will get to the point that while you're trying to
come up with a title for a writing project you're
currently working on, you may say a title name to
yourself, but one that gives you an idea for a
completely different story line.

There are several different kinds of titles. There
are titles that shock the reader, titles that surprise,
or make statements. There are titles that denote
sad or happy situations. Titles that are trick titles,
those that create questions in the mind, perhaps
dramatic titles, or titles of places. There are long
titles, and short ones. The better titles are as short
as possible and still get the message across to
the reader. Some simply need to be long. The
average title length runs from one word, to five or
six words.

When you send a story line to an editor, and you haven't settled on a title you consider the perfect title, you can label your work with a working title, then provide a list of other potential titles you have considered for the same piece.

This gives the editor a few titles for the piece that she may think might be better. Yet, it is not unusual for an editor to change your title completely, of course she can do this, she is the person selling the article to the public. You're only selling it to her.

If, when you are writing the manuscript and you can't come up with a title in the beginning, you may find it in the first few sentences, or paragraphs. If you have a manuscript that hasn't sold, perhaps it just needs a new title.

Let's say your grandparents had an old cabin out in the woods with outdoor plumbing. As a child you didn't like going to the outhouse because it had bugs all over inside. Later you write a story about it, then try to come up with a title. You could call it "The buggy place." But "The Spider House," might be better.

Endings are nearly as important as titles. This is not always the case with non-fiction, but is a good practice to follow in fiction. Both, a good title, and a good ending, will impress a reader. An ending should bring a point home about the story line, a final finish for the mind. There are no rules for endings, but there should be at least one or two. One of those rules would be that you do not use more than two or three sentences to end a story line.

Here's an example of a short, 'Point of View' newspaper story that appeared in the Peninsula Daily News in Port Angeles Washington.

THE GLINT OF LIGHT ON A SHARP NEEDLE
It's 4 a.m., and you awake to a startling sound. It's the curtains being brushed to one side, but you swear it's the soft flutter of her wings as she approaches your bedside. She is here for your blood, and as you shudder your veins shrivel from fright.

You know her as Lynn, but in your mind you refer to her as the "Vampire."

She hovers quietly over you, her needle at the ready. Then she says those soft words she has practiced in the dark of the early morning hours, day after day.

"Good morning , I'm Lynn, and I have to draw a blood sample for your morning lab work."

When you expect to spend a few days boarding at the Hospital, expect to hear the soft voice in the early hours. The voice will say, "Good Morning," and if you're quick, you might see the glint of light as it reflects off the sharp tip of the needle heading for your vein.

Lynn is part of the laboratory staff at the Hospital. These are folks who catch all the flack at the beginning of the hospital work day. This lady is the person who has to go around waking up each patient at this ungodly hour.

Lynn, and those she shares this responsibility with, have learned to be as sweet as need be, because they know you are rebellious about them sticking another needle into your arm at 4 a.m.

They work hard at what they do, each of them perfecting their ability.

Why four in the morning? Because the lab needs to get its work done before the doctors start making their rounds, and the doctors want that information available on every one of their patients.

Be gentle in the words you choose to use in your conversation with this person. She may be working to save your life.

*   *   *

The author's working title was "Rooming at the Hospital." Yet the editor exercised his right, and chose a title more to his liking from within the text, and eight words at that.

Two important things about this article, one is the opening. Immediately the reader is captivated by the question, of who is it that comes in with a "Soft flutter of her wings?"

Then the story eluding to a Vampire, draws them further into the story and they have to finish reading the entire article.

The final point is the ending. "She may be working to save your life." The story line is interesting in the beginning, and then it finishes with the reader having something to think about.

One last item, titles cannot be copyrighted, and they can be used again, and again. However, in some cases they can be trademarked.

STORY IDEAS

Many writers suggest that you keep notebooks handy for ideas as they pop into your mind because story ideas can come to you at any time. Keeping a notebook in any location where you might spend time. Keeping one at your writing desk, another one on your bedroom night table at the side of your bed, and one in your car usually covers most of the times you will need one for quick notes. Even then, you may find yourself with quick notes written on scraps of paper in your pockets. The most successful stories or book idea's often come from your own life. Not necessarily about your life, but situations, and experiences you encounter along the way.

Suppose you have someone in the family who has never gambled in their entire life, then out of the blue, a new casino is built in your vicinity. Suddenly a family member is spending their time, and the family money in the casino. You could do a story about, "The gambler among us." This kind of thing happens often when the ease to gamble becomes available. Also, it is common for someone to become addicted to gambling. Possibly someone who has never exhibited these traits before.

Perhaps you discover someone in your neighborhood that remains a recluse, even living close to the city, but rarely venturing out into the nearby area, or neighborhood.

Just ask yourself, why is this, why is that, why anything. You will begin to see the list of writing potentials is endless.

Keep in mind that the things you question others will question as well. The things you find of interest others will also find interesting, and if you find the answers others will want to read about your findings.

Knowledge is marketable, and you the writer, and aspiring author, need only to start working on your personal projects. The more you write about items of interest, the more you will recognize the potential of material you come across nearly every day.

Some of the greatest minds, whether it's writers, researchers, scientists, Astronomers, Physicists, or whatever, often start a magnificent work after reading something written by another writer.

Something a writer reads that gives him an idea, something that brings about new thoughts in his mind. Perhaps a life's work begins to form from one new mental direction started because the writer may have read about a theory. An odd situation some other writer has written about that captures his imagination.

It is common for writers to write about some story idea, then at a later time they think of another avenue for some of that same information. The new idea spurns another new direction, and on, and on. Until, the writer finally uses every possible bit of the material in one direction or another. One good idea can expand several times, each avenue different, each ongoing.

In any story line you must remember you need tension to keep a story moving, and a reader reading. This is brought about with UNCERTAINTY lingering in some manner, EMOTIONS left unchecked, or building, and reader INVOLVEMENT in the story.

In your areas of uncertainty, as soon as one problem is taken care of, a new one should replace it. In the story the protagonist needs to care in some manner as to what happens. If done correctly the reader will care as well.

While writing, see if you can feel the character's feelings while you are writing about them.

LITERARY, or COMMERCIAL FICTION
Which are you writing?
Literary fiction pays more attention to the style of writing. It probes deeper into the story's characters, and it is slower paced. As a generality this kind of fiction also has happy endings. However, this was not the case with 'Moby Dick.'

Commercial fiction can be just as well written, but in a different way. It will have a faster pace to the story. Stronger plots, more events, higher stakes, and more danger. The characterization can range from in-depth, to, non-existent. In this case, it is the story that counts not the words that tell the story.

SIDE BARS

Another market for some of your ideas would be the 'Side Bar.' This is a section of information that often accompanies the article itself. Side Bars, are the information you often see in small shaded boxes on the sides of the pages.

This is information that can be of interest to the reader, but is not part of the immediate story line. This can be facts about the content of the article that the author may have made available.

This is information that any contributing author has offered, as it is common for a writer to have sent in some work that does not quite fit as a current article material, but that can be used as a "Side Bar" in conjunction with another article already slated for publication.

In this case, both authors get published, and as a rule, both get bylines and paid for their work.

OUTLINES.

An outline generally consists of a short paragraph about each chapter. It will have the authors name, the title, the number of pages, and whether there are photographs and drawings available. You can use an entire page for each chapter if you feel the need. These include the basic content of each chapter. An example can be as simple as follows.

Outline proposal - Writing to Publish
Donald L. Boone Page 66

Chapter/Segment SASE's   1 page only.
Yes, as a writer an SASE is something you hear about all of the time, and it's an item any serious writer understands fully. "What is it?" A new writer might ask. Serious writers know that to send any of their work to an editor without including one of these valuable envelopes is courting disaster for the hours spent writing the manuscript.

Outline proposal - Writing to Publish
Donald L. Boone Page 123

Chapter/Segment TITLES   1 page only.
Titles are your key to success. They advertise your work and your ability. Followed by a paragraph that grabs the editors, and then the reader's attention. Titles can be tricky, but once mastered, they will become second nature. When you pick up a book, or a magazine, what is the first thing you look at? The titles of course.

SYNOPSIS

Okay, you've gotten a response to your query letter, and now the editor wants to see a few sample chapters, and a synopsis, or perhaps just the synopsis. This is an important tool to use in the sale of your work. A synopsis is a brief breakdown of your work, a summery of what your novel is all about.

A synopsis is a short story version of the entire manuscript and you may find writing this can be tougher than writing the book. Your editing must cast out any information that is not needed to propel the manuscript forward, yet the story line must flow smoothly. A synopsis should be kept to as few pages as possible, three or so is ideal, but not always possible.

A trick you might try in attempting to write a synopsis of any work you have finished is in a sense, similar to writing a table of contents. Each chapter you use, and you may not have to use all of them, will be a brief review of what is in that chapter. This method covers the basic plot.

When submitting your synopsis, do so in Times Roman, or Courier fonts, editors and publishers prefer size twelve fonts. It is easier to read, and double-spaced type is preferred. The margins should be the same as any manuscript. Once you have your synopsis written, take out any chapter numbers, letting each section flow into the next. To mark the beginning of a chapter, consider using a paragraph indent for each chapter, rather than a chapter number.

At the top of your first page, you need to have your name, address, telephone number, and an e-mail address if you have one. On each of the following pages you need the title, author's name, and the page number. Some writers feel each of these items has a specific location for placement. Such as the first page, your name and address in the upper left the title and your name in the center. If you have an agent, that persons name and address belongs in the lower right corner.

There are sources you can check for references in this matter. Such as the book, "Writer's Market," which is published each year, and full of this kind of information, as well as their 'Guide to Manuscript Formats.'

PROLOGS, EPILOGS, FORWARDS, and
PREFACES
A Prolog is placed in the front of the book. It is
used before the first chapter, and it explains
situations that took place prior to the current story
being told. It brings the reader up to date as to
what happened previously, and what direction
may be used to start the beginning of the story.
From this point, the book takes the reader onward
into the lives of those characters being written
about.

An Epilog is used at the back of the book to tie up
loose ends that happened during the story. This
might be the end results of some character's life
that was left hanging during the story. A part of
the book that feeds the final answers to questions
the reader may have about the outcome of
events, or of people lives.

Forwards are introductions to your work written by
others, generally authors, or those involved in
similar fields. This is an area where the author
might have someone who is well known write their
opinion of the work being presented.

A Preface is written by the author, and explains
the reason the author has chosen to write the
book. I'm to understand that this is a section that
a lot of book reviewers get their information from.

If this is the case, you want to produce good information here. In this authors case, I actually read the book I'm doing a review on.

CHECK LIST
Most story lines should have these items.

Each chapter must capture the reader's attention as early as possible, this ability is known as the hook. Then, when readers get to the end of the chapter you want to leave them wondering what is going to happen next. When you leave them wanting the answers at the end of a chapter, you don't have to tell them in the very next chapter. In the next chapter, you start a new mystery for them to wonder about and another new answer the reader wants to know about. Now perhaps you give them an answer to some previous situation that you had left dangling.

An error often made by the inexperienced writer is to supply the reader with an immediate answer about a curious event in a chapter, and just as the reader finishes that same chapter. You want the reader to keep moving through to the end of the book, so don't give them the answers ahead of time. Make that reader keep reading to find the answer later in the book.

However, when it comes to chapters you must remember if you make each chapter a story unto itself, you are writing episodes of short stories.

When the chapter ends, it must lead the reader forward, satisfied with what they have read, but unsatisfied in not knowing what lies ahead.

Paragraphs in magazine articles should have two or three sentences, maybe four, never more. This would equal roughly six typed lines. The ending of an article must re-enforce what you told the reader you would provide them with in the beginning.

Before you print your manuscript, preview your printed page by checking how it will look ahead of time. Most word processing software programs have a 'Print Preview.' ability available. If you wait until you print out a hard copy of the entire manuscript to see if you left a single line (windows, or orphans) of print at the top, or bottom of pages, you may have a problem.

If this is the copy you intend sending to a publication, you may have to print it again. Publishers hate these loose lines, and invariably a typesetter misses seeing them during the setup and then the following story line does not make sense.

It isn't always easy, but try to write the story as if you are the character, and do this for each character. Add the emotional state of the character as well.

Your story must move forward continually, if not, you can lose readers. If some part of your work seems odd, or stalled, read it again. This time look to see if you have at least one out of five sentences moving your story forward. This is a story action of some kind that moves the story along.

SHORT STORIES.
You might start writing a short story only to have it turn into a full-blown novel, or it can just as easily remain a short story. It is common to have short stories grow way beyond their original concept. As in any kind of writing, the beginnings must be catchy, and endings can be tricky, but once mastered they will find their way onto your written page.

Short stories are often composed of 'Descriptive or Creative writing.' This kind of writing is used in novels, short stories, and poetry. Its use is to create a picture for the reader to see in their mind's eye. To see the surroundings, hearing the people speak, to feel their feelings, and understand their response to the emotions involved.

As you practice your writing skills, you will find more items to write about than you thought possible.

You can reach a point in which you have so many ideas to pursue that you have to sort through them to decide which is the more important at the time.

Short stories can come out of anywhere and at anytime, day or night. They can be simple things, such as watching a child who is learning about bugs by watching ants crawling on a tree trunk. The child takes delight in their continual march out of sight. So, you write a story concerning ants.

Perhaps you are visiting the West Coast, and while watching the sun set on the distant horizon, you notice a green flash of light at the last moment. When you mention it to someone, you find it is a common occurrence. Yet, it inspires a thought for a short story.

Not surprising, but many writers come up with short stories, and sometimes complete novels, out of their dreams.

WRITING YOUR OWN NOVEL.
The wish of many writers is to write a novel.
Often, as a new writer, the awareness of how
much time a book requires on their part, and the
dedication to the project is not considered. With
this in mind, a new writer may say to themselves,
or anyone else who might care to listen. "I just
don't have the time to write."

Actually, you do have the time, but this is where
the dedication part of writing comes into play.
Just to become aware, make it a point to sit down
one day, and write one thousand words. Then
consider that if you wrote one thousand words a
day, in the course of a year, you would have three
hundred and sixty thousand words. This can be
equivalent to six novels a year. It can start by
writing a few minutes a day, even if it is only ten or
fifteen if possible.

It is common for a writer to have several things to
work on at one time, When if they get tired of
working on one project, they'll move onto a
different one. Doing this keeps the mind fresh.
Writers often have many ideas to work on, and
most can't keep all of these ideas in their minds.
So it is a good idea to make a list, or keep a note
disk for the ideas for later review.

The desire to write is the key element to a
successful writer.

You will need some idea of how to string words together, and some knowledge of the language you want to write in, as well as the genre. Notice I didn't say you had to know how to spell, or even understand the grammatical correctness of your composition. You do need to want to write.

Building characters that fulfill your story line and sounding like real people can be difficult for a person who has kept to themselves for most of their lives. A hermit learns little about the habits, or behavior patterns of other people. If, however, you are outgoing, you will have an abundance of characters you can draw upon. Even intermingling some of them for more picturesque individuals.

Consider what it is in life that motivates, or spurns your characters ahead in their life, why do they do what they are doing? You must have some kind of story facts, events, conflicts, tensions, and emotions to deal with. What is it the characters want to accomplish, and what is the outcome of their actions. Most books require at least two characters, and five or six characters are not out of line. Ten or twelve may tax the reader's memory, even losing some readers.

In the writing of your book, consider that the first phase will encompass about thirty percent of the book. It will be used to develop the characters, any needed descriptions, and the basic plot. The second phase of your book will use nearly fifty percent of the book's volume. This is the part where the conflict takes place, the action here is faster than the first portion. The last phase is the remaining twenty percent, and is the final resolution. When the end takes place, it takes place.

CHILDREN'S BOOKS.
To write in this field the author must understand the young mind. In this market you direct your work toward various youthful age groups and the language of those age groups. Regarding children's books, the author may have little to say about the illustrations they feel the book should have, as publishers generally have artists that they use for any illustrations they publish. These may be freelance artists, or staff personnel.

Story ideas come from the writer's mind and imagination, they are not born in the minds of others then transmitted through the writer's mind for refinement. Children's stories come from the depths of memories, and young experiences. Some children's stories have plots, many don't. Nearly all have moral issues imbedded in them and some start out as a single story, and some seem to grow into additional stories.

Make your more important story parts longer than the less important. This is an easy item to forget.

THE CHILDREN'S MARKET
Writers Markets / Jan. 2000

Genre	Grade level	typewritten pages
Picture book	Toddler – Grade 4	2 – 10
Easy Reader / Beginning Chapter book	K – 3	15 – 25
Young Chapter book	2 – 4	30 – 50
Middle Grade Novels	3 – 7	60 – 150
Young Adult Novels	8 – 12	150 – 300
Magazine	Toddler – 12	1 – 5
Nonfiction	Toddler – 12	2 – 300
Poetry	Toddler – 12	1

According to two different reports, one stated that in 1950 children 14 years old, had a vocabulary of 25,000 words, another stated that in 1950 children leaving high school had a vocabulary of 14,000 words. In the year 2000, the 14-year-old child had a vocabulary of 10,000 words. If either report is correct, then our children have lost at least 4,000 to 15,000 words.

With texting is on the rise on the internet, the ability to spell is becoming a problem of major proportions.

CHAPTERS WHAT LENGTH?

This can be a controversial subject, who's to say how long, or how short a chapter is to be. As an example, the chapter length found in most books is about 250 words per double spaced page, or 500 words per single spaced page. This indicates that chapters can be anywhere from one page to a lengthy chapter of fifteen pages. A comfortable reading length is about half of that, or six or seven pages.

Most people who read a great deal prefer to have chapters of a length where they become easy places to stop when they tire of reading. Most readers dislike picking up the book they are currently immersed in, and having to start in the middle of a chapter. When this happens, they have to remember what has taken place in the story previously. When they are about to begin reading again, they may refer back a page or two, to get back into the story line of the chapter.

The preference, is that the reader wants to start fresh on a new section with new thoughts. This is also one of the reasons why the writer needs to draw them in, in each new chapter, then leaving the reader hanging mentally until the next chapter.

Recently, while speaking with a woman in search of a freelance editor to look at her book, she explained that her book is forty five thousand words in length, and contains only seven chapters.

This means each chapter is about seven or eight thousand words in length. To some readers, a fifteen page chapter is not a really a chapter but more of a short story. Perhaps each of them even qualifying as a Novella'.

Chapters are natural breaks in the story line. A location where a writer can take license to add something which seems totally unrelated to the previous chapter, yet will be used to explain another situation that will happen later in the book.

Perhaps an 'Expository subject,' worked into the story line to inform and clarify something for the reader. A forewarning in a sense that a situation will appear later in the story. A primer for something that if left unsaid may cause the reader to question the author's work, or subject matter later in the story line.

While sitting in your writers group, look around at the others, and listen to the small stifled moans when you hear a writer declare, "Yes, I am ready to read part of my latest work. Today I'm reading chapter seven in my book titled, "Good heavens." This chapter is twenty-two pages long and I . . . ."

When she said twenty-two pages you can bet many eyes rolled up in their sockets. Consider this, if you have long, long chapters, perhaps you're not writing, but rambling.

WRITING AND SELLING MAGAZINE ARTICLES. Okay you've spent hours, perhaps days perfecting something you have written, and now you would like to see it published. Maybe you have even found the correct market for your manuscript. So off it goes in the mail, and happily you receive a note from the editor saying she wants to use it in the next issue.

Once you have sold your work to an editor and its been published, you might want to consider sending a sample list of other work you have available to that same publisher, or editor.

This would be a list of potential article information you can provide for that same publication, and these will be items that fit into their current publishing needs. These work samples are to be the main body of this samples page but are listed on a separate piece or piece of paper. These pages also need to include your name, address, and telephone number.

A sample list is comprised of short summaries of each piece you're offering the publication. Be sure to include a word count for each piece, also photo's that may be available, or drawings.

These short sample summaries must contain hooks in the story line to grab the reader and the editor. The sample list you send can include reprints, or second rights, but that information should be mentioned on the heading of each piece being offered to the editor.

Another twist is in marketing your work on the global market. In the international market you must remove anything that Americanizes your work, or the removal of any indications leading to a particular nation. Why, because your views are not always reflected, or accepted, in the same manner in other counties. If your work is useful, it can find a market, but it must be appealing to everyone.

There are several markets open for the writer, it is the writer who must do their homework to find the market for their material. One of the best places to check for markets is with your own library. Ask the librarian what she recommends as to locating books or magazines in print, and then, tell her thank you.

One more thought along these lines, you might want to read a few of the story leads and the openings, to see what the editor is currently buying. Also to see what is grabbing the readers attention in your chosen publications.

You might sell some of your work to selected publications if you pitch an idea that ties in with an upcoming theme for that publication. Upcoming theme? Yes. Most magazines plan at least a year in advance of what they are going to publish and some of them have particular themes they follow. If you query the publication, they will often provide you with the next year's theme ahead of time.

This information then puts you, the writer, in a position to send work that fits the publication's needs, and can put your work on a higher priority slush pile. It also tells the editor, that here is an author doing their homework, and your name may get jotted down somewhere, and an opening may have just been created to look at your work. Don't wait too long.

WHERE'S THE MONEY?

The romantic notion that writers are rich, is a myth. A few authors do very well, but compared to the multitude of writers who are writing, it's very few. In some cases an author may spend years collecting data for a book, in the end that same author has to consider if the time spent was worth the amount of royalties received.

Consider this scenario, an author collects notes and theories on a subject of interest over a period of ten years. Finally reaching a point where the author has accumulated enough information to write a book about that subject.

The book becomes published, and the first printing is five thousand copies. The author nets five hundred dollars for this first printing in royalties. This means the author makes about one dollar and four cents a week for the ten year period of time spent in getting the data together for the book, or four dollars and sixteen cents a month.

Yet this same author can sit down at the word processor keyboard and spend about an hour, maybe two. Writing a magazine article which may bring a check from one hundred, to three hundred dollars for first rights. Perhaps rewritten once or twice for additional first rights and then the author begins selling the same pieces for second rights.

This means the one, to three hundred dollar magazine article can eventually bring in six hundred to better than a thousand dollars. That's not bad wages for a couple of hour's work.

There are books which seem to go together much faster than the one mentioned above, some may only take months in putting a first draft together. Most often the information in these books has been accumulating in the author's mind for some time. In addition the author may have all the needed data available to fill out the required number of words for this book to satisfy the publisher's needs.

This kind of book is very self satisfying to the author, mainly because the book is easily written, and will bring in some royalties for the author's bank account.

The question is this, Which author are you? The author who writes books in a hurry, and then markets the work, or the long term writer? You can of course, do both kinds of books.

You have decide where the money is to be made. Magazine articles are easier to write, take less time, produce income faster, and in less time. Having books published is fun, but will it put money in your bank account fast enough to suit you?

POETRY

For those of you who are writing Poetry, and want to see it published, you must understand it is the toughest market to break into. Poetry is a very personal manner of writing. The better poetry does not keep the meanings of the poem hidden; it shows it to the world.

AVERAGE DAILY MINUTES SPENT READING BY AGE BRACKETS.

Age	1990 - 2000
Under 25	24
25 – 29	24
30 – 34	28
35 – 39	31
40 – 44	35
45 – 49	41
50 – 54	44
55 – 64	53
65 – 75	60
75 – 85	120 - 240

THE AVERAGE LENGTH IS ....?
Approx. No.

Double-spaced	Average Words	Pages
Chapters	75 – 3800	3 - 10
Short-short story	500 – 2,000	2 - 8
Short-story	2,500 – 5,000	10 - 20
Novella	7,500 – 40,000	30 - 160
Novelette	7,000 – 25,000	28 – 100
Novel: hard cover	25,000 – 150,000	100 - 600
Novel: paperback	35,000 – 80,000	140 - 320
Children's Picture Book	2,500 – 5,000	2 - 10
Juvenile book	15,000 – 80,000	60 - 320
Nonfiction book	20,000 – 200,000	80 - 800

TV script: ½ hour	25 - 40
TV script: 1 hour	55 - 70

Play: one act 20 – 30 min. playing time. 20 - 30
Movie   1-1/2 – 2 hrs. playing time.   120 - 150

Radio feature copy   1 min. = 15 double-spaced
lines

Radio feature copy   3 min. = 2 pages

Poem 2 – 100 lines, most magazines prefer 4 –
16 lines

Query letters,   1 full page, single-spaced.
                  2 pages for a book.

Speech   250 words = 2 min.
                12 – 15 pages = ½ hour

NOTE: These page counts are based upon 500 words per page. You can adjust these finding by your personal word count per page.

One last note. How long are paragraphs? They are anywhere from one, to four sentences in length. Read your newspaper, you will find the paragraphs are only one, or two sentences in length.

WRITING IN VARIOUS DIRECTIONS
When you consider that 37% of all books sold, and 53% of all paperbacks sold, are romance novels, it may make you think about writing for one of these genre's. Of which there are at least five different basic types. However, there are several different kinds of writing that a writer can investigate for potential fields of endeavor. Many magazine freelance writers often write for many different magazines all at the same time, and in different categories, and genres.

TIME SENSITIVE ARTICLES.
These are articles that favor a certain time of year. Such as Christmas, Thanksgiving, Halloween, Valentines Day, etc. This kind of article needs to be in the editor's hands about six months in advance. In a manner of speaking, most holiday story lines are worn out. Editors cringe at the thought of having to come up with something new each season. Think about it, is there really any new way of saying "I love you," on Valentines Day. Most likely there is, and any editor is open to hear it from you. These are easily sold pieces if you have a new slant for these well worn holidays.

ONCE YOU'RE ESTABLISHED.

If your work begins to show up less on the printed page in one of your favored publications, consider sending a personal note to your editor, such as the following.

F. R. Hiccup – Editor
Frank, I've noticed the lack of my work, and similar writing subjects appearing in your publication recently. What can I do for you to correct this trend?

There might be several reasons, such as the publication changing themes, or just seasonal material. Perhaps your work no longer fits into their currently required needs. If this is the case, and you can change to their needs, consider doing so.

FOLLOWING UP.

Follow up letters to editors or publishers can be an important item in your writing schedule, and this is another reason you should keep track of where your work is, and what rights have been offered.

The tacking method you use should be a listing of which editor, and which publication has each piece of material at any given point in time.

Editors are very busy people, and it is common or an editor to get so wrapped up in the current publication, that he overlooks other things that need his attention, and that o be placed in upcoming issues. You can occasionally jog the editors memory, and after a reasonable time period, if you haven't heard from him, consider sending a follow up letter. If your follow up letter does not find its way to the editor in a timely fashion, you can miss out on potential sales.

When you should send a follow up letter, is a matter of self-decision. In reading the publication's writer's guidelines, you will normally find the guidelines specify when you should expect to hear from the publication regarding your manuscript. f you do not receive some kind of response within that time frame. I would suggest that after the period has elapsed give it a few more days then send a quick note similar to the one below.

However, do not become a follow up letter pest, send one letter at your chosen time, and then wait long enough for the editor to respond. Also you should send another SASE with your follow up letter, this makes it even easier for the editor to get back to you, and odds are the editor will be scrambling through his files in search of your work.

Sample follow up letter.
Your name and address.

THE EDITOR'S NAME. – EDITOR
TRUE CONFESSIONS
Mac Fadden Women's Group
233 Park Avenue South
New York, NY 10003
Good morning
'm inquiring about the article titled, "THE GHOST."
I sent to you in January of this year. It concerns a
period of my daughter's life, and her obsession
with a younger man. She didn't realize she was
obsessed with him until nearly thirty years had
passed.

Finally a family related event brought it to mind,
and to a point where she understood that it had
been an obsession. After the self-confrontation,
she was finally able to let the obsession die. Now
it is just a ghost from the past, thank goodness.
Thank you.

Mrs. Author

The article had been placed in the Editor's desk
drawer for consideration, then forgotten.

EDITORS OF ANOTHER KIND.
There is an odd type of editor we should talk about. This is the NEEDY EDITOR, well in a sense they are all needy.

A publishers and editors require new books, or story ideas for magazines to offer the reading public. If they do not get them, they have a serious problem, they are out of business.

This is the situation whereas you, the writer are offered a chance to get published in your chosen publication, or by your chosen publisher. Of course you probably knew this didn't you? And, you knew this is why editors are constantly in need of new material.

Yet, there is an editor who is really searching for new writers, and she knows these writers will have the material she is looking for. This editor works for a publisher who handles unusual reading material. This would be the specialized fields. Such as the different Sciences, Technical trades, Astronomical, Astrological, Theological, only to name a few.

So you're thinking, 'I can't write something like that, I've only done fingernails at the beauty salon for the past fifteen years,' or 'I've only been a nurse for the past . . . ., I've only been a legal secretary. . . . ., I've only been a housewife all my life. . .' and on it goes.

Well think again, odds are you're an expert and didn't realize the potential of you knowledge.

Maybe you think of odd questions that might sell to an odd magazine, such as 'What was Jimmy really doing when he cracked corn.' Or 'Why do black olives come in cans, and green olives come in jars.' You see, if you use your mind, there are lots of things to write about that are of interest to someone, and you can get paid for this kind of thinking.

So what to do, you find the editor looking for odd, or specialized stuff, write it, and send it to your future.

SELF PUBLISHING.
This can be a hard decision to make. On one
hand, if you self publish your work, you stand to
make all of the money from the publication, and
not just royalties. At the same time, you can lose
everything you invest in the book as well.
Marketing is the key factor here, and the book
must be marketable. If a regular publisher or
editor finds fault with it, the problems must be
corrected.

I'd recommend a book titled, "THE COMPLETE
GUIDE TO SELF-PUBLISHING," By Tom &
Marilyn Ross. This is one of the better books on
this subject. ISBN 0-89879-354-8 published in
1989. Also, I recommend you have someone with
the savvy look it over from a reader's viewpoint.
Such as a freelance editor, or one or two trusted
friends. I say trusted friends, because you need
the truth, not what they think you want to hear that
and you want them to remain friends.

SUBSIDY PUBLISHERS.
This is nearly the same as self-publishing. A subsidy publisher does the work for you, but does not market your work. You still have to do the selling. Though the work may be much more professionally done, depending upon your own abilities of course, and the cost of printing the book still comes out of your pocket.

However, there is another method of self publishing that has been made available to writers. The ones I can think of at the moment that I am familiar with are "CreateSpace.com' also, "LuLu.com" If you go with CreateSpace your booiks can be sold on Amazon.com. A key factor for self publishing now, and at this point, is being able to save files in HTML as well as PDF formats. Doing so will allow you to market your books in the E-books markets. Such as Kindle, Nook Books, Google Books, and others.

POETRY
For those of you who are writing Poetry, you must understand that this is the toughest market to break into. I suggest you read any magazines pertaining to writers you can find in the library. Quite often you will find listings for publications that accept poetry, and you often find contests for Poets in these same publications.

WORD COUNT.
Most word processors contain a word counting
option. Look under your tool bar at the top of your
computer screen. You should have a spot labeled
as "TOOLS." Right click this with your mouse
button, and select the Word Count heading.

Another method is to count the words in six lines,
then divide that total by six. This will give you the
average words per sentence. Multiply this number
by the amount of sentences on the page for the
word count for that page. Multiply this number by
the amount of pages in the book, for a general
idea of the total word count.

GALLEYS

Receiving 'Galleys' for one of your books is always enjoyable, no matter how many books you have written, or how many you've had published. They also present you, the author, with a lot of work to be done and in a short period of time. You have read this material over, and over, and over, but now you need to do it one last time. This time you read very slowly and very methodical, as if you are reading it for the first time.

Some of the problems arise when the publisher has to change the format from the files you sent to them. Most often your work has been written on a word processing program other than the one the publisher uses for setting up the type setting for your book. Even the slightest incompatibility can be disastrous to the printed page format.

When you review the galleys sent to you by your publisher, you must read it word for word, and number for number, especially if it is a textbook of any kind. To do so will reveal additional letters, or numbers in places where they do not belong, nor do they make any sense where they now reside. Often this will be found where a quotation mark, (") now appears as a (▯) instead. Or perhaps a (§) in a place where you had some other kind of marking. These are only two of many.

When you save a file from your word processor to a PDF, or HTML file, then view it as a book, you will find a problem you may not understand. An example of this would be how much an left tab can mess up a list you expected to fit on a page. In this case dots or dashes work better to achieve the needed space. Of course if you are using a word processor that does not allow you to see the codes your word processor inserts into your document, you may struggle to find the problem.

You will find some lines of information have slipped out of place, which will require they be moved left or right, on occasion you will find completely blank pages inserted in the manuscript for no apparent reason. Whatever the error, you the author are responsible for noting these errors, and getting that information to the editor and publisher.

Check to be sure that if you make a reference in the book to another location in the book that, that same information can be found. Often the publisher will just do a print out hard copy of the book, then this is what is sent to you for a final approval. If you, the author, do not find the errors your reading public will. Then the publisher will mention them to you, and you won't feel comfortable when you hear the news no matter how polite the editor seems to be about the situation.

What the publisher sends to you as a galley will be the finished product no matter the errors if you do not take the time to read through it carefully.

The publisher will send a note saying, "Read through the galley and make any notes or changes in red ink." Heed this note, and do as the publisher requests.

An idea that works well for both parties, you and the publisher, is a detailed list that you compile as you read through the galley.

As you read through the galley, make any notes on the galley copy you like, but on separate sheets of paper, make additional notes of corrections, changes of any kind. Referring to page numbers, paragraphs, sentences, or lines of text. You make two copies of these notes.

When you are finished reading through your galley the second or third time, and are satisfied you have found every problem, then type up a corresponding list of those problems. This list you send back to the publisher with the galley, and another copy goes into your personal file.

PRINTING INFORMATION.
For those of you who might be seeking prices for having some of your work done by a printer, you can obtain a good idea of prices for this service by asking if Gorham Printing will send you their catalog. When last I spoke with a representative from this company, the catalog is 68 pages in length. It is a very good cross section of printing needs you might require.

BOOK PRINTING PRICES and information from GORHAM PRINTING.1999
Info@gorhamprinting.com

MISCELLANEOUS INFORMATION

Merging files.

It is common to have problems between the software your word processor uses, and that of your editor, or publishing house. We've discussed these problems before, so we'll not repeat those situations again. However, you, as the writer can make it even more difficult without even trying.

Consider this condition, you are one of those writers who have two or more word processing software packages installed on your computer. The main reason for doing this is to make it easier to write the piece in the same format that the editor of your choice prefers to use.

The hazard comes about because of this very ability. What can happen, and often does, is that you write something in one software format, then decide at a later date that some of the information can be used in another story line. Perhaps the item you are currently writing is in WordPerfect, and you want some material you wrote in Microsoft Word.

You open a new page over the current file you are working on, then you go looking for a file that you recall has some information you want to use in the file you have open. You finally find it located in a file that you wrote in one of your other word processing systems. You open the story and select the material you desire. Once you have it selected, you copy it to the clipboard and close the program. Back in your current working file, you simply paste the item you copied into your chosen location. Now you're thinking, "Wal'la, done."

Wrong again, and here is the problem. Now you may have two different font programs involved in one story line. Not only is it possible they are incompatible with each other, but neither one of them may be compatible with your editor. The result can be chaotic. You send a copy of the work to the editor, perhaps on a floppy diskette, or a flash drive, maybe even just an attachment in an e-mail.

Just as the editor finally discovers that she seems to have a font problem, she really has no idea it is two font problems she has gotten from you. But when she finds out, guess who gets it back to fix, and will she be wary of your next work, you can count on this being the case.

SELF PUBLISHING 'WEB' INFORMATION."

You might look at

Amazon.com

CreateSpace.com

LuLu.com

Xlibris.com

lightingPrint.com

fatbrain.com/ematter/home.html

1stbooks.com

Parapublishing.com

You must remember, I'm only passing this information on to you, I am not by any means recommending any of these institutions to you. These are just sources of information that may interest you. Also, they may be current, or they can just as easily be locations of the past by the time you read this.

WRITER'S GROUPS.

I have found that belonging to a writers group can be a very helpful source of feedback for your work. Yet, others will tell you that writer's group's are a waste of time. The custom in most writers' groups is to read your work to the other writer's, and expect to receive their critique. You will find that some people do better at reading along with the writer as he/she reads their work to the group, others do better just to listen.

The individuals, who read along, often pick up writing errors in the manuscript, the ones who listen can tell if the story line flows smoothly. You, the writer, benefit from both. Remember that constructive criticism is normally welcome, but degrading, or put down criticism is not. Normally, in a writer's group, you will, and should, get constructive criticism.

Yet, writer's groups can have a slightly negative side as well, depending on your point of view. In nearly every writers group, especially those with older writers, you will have at least one person who is there for the social gathering.

They may bring something to read it could be a short poem, a piece of personal history, biography, something. Often their work shows little imagination, or color, because they are not there to receive criticism, they are there to visit.

I'm sure there are others out there, but I have only met one writer who writes their memoirs in such a manner as to be of interest to any reader, family or friend.

What's the negative side? You say. The negative is that the writer who attends purely for the social function is not normally a contributing factor in the group. Unless they have some special talent from the past, such as a wordsmith, editorial background, linguist, or some value that benefits the group.

Unless you screen those who want to join your writers group carefully, you will end up with someone who contributes little to the group. On the other hand, if you join a group already in progress, you can expect this situation to be in place on your arrival.

Don't misunderstand my concern in this matter, it's okay to have these folks in a writer's group, but you will notice the lack of participation in some manner. In that same line of thinking, a group that is all business, and little social interchange, will be dull and uninteresting.

Then, there is the group who insists on taking strict turns in reading their work, and very business like in their dealing, they will have strict rules about the interchange of criticism, who reads first, second, third, where they meet, and when they meet. Strict rules can abound, strict rules, and more strict rules. A group that is this tight does not work well together for very long. It will lose members, leaving the organizer wondering why?

Courtesy needs to be exercised in writing groups. As an example, one person brings a chapter to read that is three pages long, another writer brings a chapter that is twenty-two pages long. Whom do you want to listen too? A chapter that is twenty-two pages long, is not a chapter, it's a short story.

There is another kind of writer's group member that can make you wonder about their value to the group. This is a writer who is published and learned the tricks to becoming published. Yet within the group, this same writer offers little in the matter of punctuation, or grammatical correctness. Perhaps even their spelling leaves something to be desired. This kind of writer may be of more value in simply reading the story for a personal evaluation. Often you will find this kind of person can tell you what will work, where it will work and when. They can also tell you why it won't work. So, the question is, "Are they of value to the group?" You bet they are.

CRITICISM.

Everyone should learn to handle criticism, and as a writer, you must learn to handle criticism, and you have to learn how to interpret it as well. It may be easier if you learn to be somewhat mechanical, perhaps even cold of heart in your approach to criticism, and it will then become easier. Consider who is offering the critique, is it constructive or destructive? Criticism can make or break a new writer's spirit if they let it affect their personal feelings.

If you are a writer that carries a chip on your shoulder, criticism can be devastating. Keeping an open mind about it can carry you forward. In your mind you, the author, must determine whether it is good or bad criticism.

Writer's groups are the best source for criticism, because you are all headed in the same direction. Generally, each member of the group will follow through a copy of your work while you read it to them. At the end of your reading, each will provide written and oral comments on your work. This is constructive criticism.

Don't throw out that paragraph or chapter just because someone says it doesn't fit well where you have it. Consider rewriting the work so it fits better, or even moving that entire section of text to a better spot in the manuscript. If it is a good thought, it can be used somewhere.

When you use family or friends as readers for criticism, you should remember most readers do not understand how to critique. Choose your readers carefully, and then, in the end, ask pertinent questions of them. Ask them how the grammar was, how about the spelling, the punctuation, correct word usage, are the characters realistic, and did the story flow well.

Doing it this way will provide honest answers. If asked incorrectly, you will lead the reader into giving you answers they think you want to hear. Never argue with one of your readers, if you do, you may never get them to read for you again, and if they do, their answers will be tainted.

Can you edit your own work, yeah! Sure you can.

When you get a gathering of writers together, you are entering a hot bed of egos.

WRITER'S RESUME

And just when you thought you were done with presenting resumes. Still. as a writer, it pays to have one. No! not a resume of your social vocational work history, but a resume of your writing history and that of your writing credentials.

Though you may not be well published yet, this can come about if you want it too. It only takes the personal drive to bring it fruition. When you reach the point of being well published, and this happens, you may actually reach a period of trying to decide which information to leave off your resume.

To the new writer, it might look something like the one below.

WRITER'S RESUME

Janice Block
1234 Front ST.
Somewhere USA, zip
e-mail address
Phone number ?

June 2012

To whom it may concern:

Previously I was the editor for the college
newsletter for Peninsula College in Port Angeles
Washington.

I am occasionally published in two local
newspapers. The Peninsula Daily News. - Port
Angeles, WA Also, the now out of print, "Looking
Ahead" – Carlsborg, WA.

I have also been published in 'Horse manure
quarterly.' An environmental magazine for the
northwest.

I currently write in my home office, and can be
reached via my E-mail address, or by telephone.

Janice Block

COMPUTERS.

Many new writers start out by trying to keep ideas in their heads until they can write them down, or type them on paper. At some point, they come to understand they are collecting too many ideas to keep in their heads, and need to make a few notes instead. Then those scribbled notes are placed into a file, and this file eventually gets slipped into a box. Often a transition to using notebooks takes place, but in the end, a serious writer who wants to compete to become a published writer, must be encouraged to purchase a word processor.

As advanced as we are in most of the world, many people, who have not used a computer, distrust them. Often the older the person, the more distrust in these fancy gadgets. Computers are here to stay, and you the writer must adapt to this fact. You can purchase some word processors that resemble a typewriter, and any more they have the ability to use computer flash drives, Compact disks, and though they are used less now than before, diskettes are still around. Any device that can be used for the storage of the writer's work. Now a professional writer needs, or nearly requires a good computer with a good word processor program.

The more advanced programs offer many avenues of magic for the writer. Magic that most publishers now require the writer to take advantage of. Especially when sending work to them for their consideration. Another advantage to the more sophisticated programs, is the ability to store vast amounts of information in several formats on different storage devices. All of this can be done normally and without fear of losing that information. In the past I've only had two of the three and a half-inch computer diskettes fail in over ten years of writing, and I still have hundreds of these diskettes. As far as flash drives, I understand they can fail for storage after and extended period. If they become full of fragmented junk, you can't clear them out. I think this is what happens.

For the typing impaired, there are software programs available which allow you to dictate, and talk to your computers word processing program. The financial cost of these programs are reasonable in price, and take little effort to program them to your voice and word style.

Also, there are software programs available that provide translation to and from most other languages. And most computer word processor programs have several keyboard layouts which allow a user to write in another language.

You will hear all kinds of information, such as what computer system someone should purchase for their home use, and the answer is different for each of us.

There are several kinds of systems available, but you should choose one that is the most compatible with other systems.

Most writers use a system that is known a 'IBM compatible.' This is not to say you should purchase an IBM computer, just one that is compatible with that kind of computer system. The reason is because an IBM compatible computer has a much larger availability of software programs that can be used on your system, that of your aunt, uncle, brother, sister, or more importantly, your editor.

It used to be imperative to have a computer in which the memory could be upgraded to a higher level. This is not the case any longer. Most off the shelf computers, Laptops, or Towers, have more storage space than you will ever likely find a use for. Also, they will allow anything you want to add to the system through what is known as. "Plug and Play."

As writer, you will also need a good printer, and the computer system will normally include a mouse, which is a hand held pointing device, though there are several types that now allow you to control your computer on a remote basis. Good keyboards are common place, and of course you will need a printer as well. Once you become aware of how you computer works, and get used to keeping your work saved on a storage device you may want to do so every fifteen minutes or so. During stormy weather, you may want to save your work more often. Most word processor programs can be set to save your work automatically every few minutes, and may save it when a power outage takes place.

Editors expect their writers to use a number 12 size font. For those of you who do not know how to set your computer fonts to this size, you do this with MS word. Select FORMAT on your toolbar, then select FONT. You will have a FONT window drop down, and you will need to choose NEW COURIER, then the font style REGULAR. Now under SIZE, select 12. At the bottom of the window, select the DEFAULT button. You will get a screen asking of you want this as your default font. Simply select YES. From this point on, everything you write will be in this style.

Two good things you should do to your computer every couple of months is to first run your SCAN DISK program. Or it may now be called, DISK CLEANUP. Then run your DEFRAGMENTATION PROGRAM. Using these two items can speed up your computer by cleaning up garbage you may have caused un-wittingly.

To get to these items, in Windows go to your START key, then select the PROGRAMS, then ACCESSORIES, finally SYSTEM TOOLS. When you get to this stage be sure to run your SCAN DISK, or DISK CLEANUP program first, and then the Defragmenter.

WRITER'S SECRET NOTES

It is common for writers to put stuff on paper, stuff that they would not want others to read. Why would they do this? To keep notes that have information they may want to use at a later date. Also to keep from losing the data, and yet to keep the feelings available about the way things were at a time of importance.

This would be general notes to themselves, but situations that could unlock unknown secrets about life. This does not always have to be secrets it could just be notes of interest to them as a writer.

There are different ways to do this, you can just keep them on a storage device and keep it put away. Or, at least out of sight, or you can password protect the data in the file. Of course you might have someone say, "Why do you need to keep me from reading the stuff you have in those files?" Guess who this question is coming from.

Or, you can use a hidden file attributes. In newer computers this may not be readily available, so check in your help files by pressing the (F1) key.

Some of the things you may want to keep on this device will be the hardest things to write about. So, what are the toughest thing to write about? Emotions, Love and lust

Lets discuss your vocabulary for a few moments. This is something you don't want to change, at least not consciously. It will change anyway, but let it happen naturally.

Yes, believe it or not, even your grammar will change, and most likely improve. There are a couple of books you might want to have in your personal library. "Elements of Style." By William Strunk. Also, consider "Woe is I." By Patricia O'Conner.

You will know when your writing gets better, because it will take others longer to find anything wrong with your work.

VOCABULARY

If you want to find out your personal average vocabulary, though it may make you angry, count how many of the words in the following list that you know, or understand. Following this list, is a table that will provide a probable vocabulary range.

abrasive	doubloon	maelstrom
sampan	aegis	Jclat
marinade	scraggy	alleviation
emblematical*	melodramatic	shaveling
anise	equivocation	metamorphic
shelly*	archenemy	exorcise
milliard	shillelagh	attribution
fascia	modicum	simulation
bambino	flabbergast	mossback
snuffle	beechen*	forgather
nabob	spheroid	besprent*
fructification	necromancer	stethoscope
bigamous	gaby*	nonpareil
subservience	binomial	genital
offing	surrogate	buckram
gondolier	oubliette	tabard
calender	grunter	padrone
tannery	carom	hansom*
participator	therapy	chaffer
herbivorous	perforation	tocsin
cloister	hornbeam	pickaback
trefoil	cochineal	hypotheses
plumbago	tyro	collusive
inadmissible	pottle	unchartered
complainant	indubitable	prioress

urbane	constitutionality	internationalist
psychiatry	vesicle	cosine
jamb	quiescent	waggle
daguerreotype	kapok	rearrangement
well-disposed	demagnetize	laminate
reimburse	wimple	devourer
leukocyte	revocation	yachting
disembowel	lodgment	rotund
zodiacal		

The words with an asterisk (*) after them could not be found in my dictionary for verification.

Words you know in the list above
Your probable vocabulary would be.

100	.50,000 or more.
90	40,000
80	30,000
70	25,000
60	20,000
50	15,000
40	12,000
30	10,000

These figures come from the book, 'The Technique of Clear Writing.' By Robert Gunning. Copyright 1968, McGraw-Hill.

CONTRACTS.

A contract can be a simple agreement such as, "I can offer you $ XX dollars for your work titled 'Good stuff' for our next publication, or the issue due out on ?? 2015."

As a contract that may be all you get. It is up to you, the author, to determine if you agree to this simple offer. From this kind of agreement you have no idea what rights you are selling or those that you retain.

Normally this kind of offer comes from a publication you have been established with as a contributing writer, and they, and yourself already understand what rights are in place. Sometimes a price may not even be mentioned, as that arrangement is also established on prior work you've offered to them. This is a common event if your work is used in a specific column, or area in the publication.

Some magazines may consider that if you send them a manuscript for their consideration, that you are in fact entering into a contractual agreement to let them publish your work. This would be an unspoken, unwritten agreement. It may only be a matter of discussing money and the rights being offered. With this in mind, it is a multiple submission it is imperative of you to let them know this fact up front.

Contracts can vary from publication to publication. You may get something as similar to this.

SOPWITH CAMEL WORKS
123 West fifth street.
Somewhere USA. Zip no.

Jimmy Doolittle
I can offer you XXXX dollars for your work titled "Air Craft Carrier Landings." If this is acceptable to you we intend to publish it on Month/day/year.

Editor so and so.

On the other hand, you might find yourself reading a two, three or four page contractual agreement with all the therefore's and wherefore's involved. These you should read entirely. If you disagree with something in the contract be sure you contact the editor and explain your concerns.

Sometimes a general contract can be modified with little concern to the editor, or the publisher. Why, You ask? Well odds are this is another standard form they have on file in their office. They've used it since they started in this business, and will continue to use it. This doesn't mean they won't bend in their demands, it also doesn't mean they will either.

Book contracts are a whole different world. These you must read carefully. Be sure you understand all of your responsibilities, and those of the publisher. They will be spelled out in the contract. You can bet on the fact that in your more lengthy contracts, especially for books, that the contract will contain a clause that states that you are the original owner of the work you have presented. In short they want a guarantee that you are the originator of the material you have sent to them. Also you will find a section that specifies what rights they want from you. When it comes to magazine articles, normally they only ask for one time North American rights.

Don't be fooled, some will ask for all rights. They ask for all rights in case they want to use the work again at a later date and cannot locate the author. You should get paid again if they can find you, but don't count on it. It may only be a reprint, or second rights payment, and about half of the original payment for the work. It's not as bad as it sounds when you give them all rights. You can use the same material again, as long as you use it in a different context, or in a different slant. This is a matter you should discuss with any editor who wants "All rights." Then be sure you keep a copy of this correspondence for you files.

Book contracts often spell out the fact that the material you have included in your book, and that they are going to publish, cannot be used elsewhere. Though you, as the author, can use the same information, it must still be used differently. Should you use the same material elsewhere, you can hurt the sales of your own book and why would you do that?

An item the publisher may require from you the author, will be holding you responsible for taking care of registering the work with the copyright office.

A contractual event that often escapes notice, by authors and publishers, is the inclusion of electronic rights in a book contract. Magazines use this option often, but you, the author will receive compensation for any of your work sold over the Internet. It may not be much, but it will be something. Be sure you understand this agreement with your publisher.

Once you are well established with an editor, or publisher, you may not get a contract when you send stuff in on speculation. If you send something unsolicited to an editor with whom you have a long-standing relationship, it may become an unwritten agreement of what you expect to be paid for the work you send. It might be four hundred words, it might be two thousand words, and the payment will be the same for either piece.

It is common to sell the same work four or five times, maybe more. This can be done by writing the same information but to a different audience, and with a different slant.

When it involves books, you the author will be given a galley copy, or Proof copy to check over before publication. This copy is for you to look over and to be certain all is in the proper order, and believe me you want to do this carefully. Any omissions or errors on your part are accepted if you okay the galley copy and do not spell out errors to the publisher before going to print.

The following is a sample contract for a book.
CONTRACT (Sample only)
The publications name here
Their address
The state and zip code

Mr. Whomever.
This contract constitutes our agreement to publish
you book (working title,). This book contains
information text and graphics, relative to the title.
The following are the terms of this contract and
the agreement between THIS PUBLICATION
(herein referred to as the publisher) and
(hereinafter referred to as the author).

(1)The changes noted by the publisher must be
made by the author within 30 calendar days of
receipt by the author and returned to the publisher
by US Priority Mail, E-mail, or Fax.

(2)The author will supply all the graphics he/she
has available for this book as part of the
manuscript.

B&W photos should be 5 X 7 or smaller, or
digitized.

Line art should be on white paper with black ink or
digitized.

(3)One B&W or color photo of the author will be
supplied by the author.

(4)The publisher will supply a color photo or art
work for the books cover.

(5)The author will supply a photo or line art for the
cover.

(6)The author will supply a 250 word autobiography.

(7)The book (working title,) will have a retail cover price of (dollars / cents) for our standard binding. If released in mass market (paperback), hard cover or other binding the retail price will be adjusted accordingly.

(8)The author's royalty of ???% will be based upon the final retail cover price of any copy, binding, edition or press run.

(9)The author will receive (XX) copies of each edition of the book without cost. Two must be used by the author to satisfy the copyright office requirements.

(10)The author may purchase up to 30 copies at a (XX%) discount off retail. Additional copies, (over XX) may be purchased at 40% discount off retail price.

(11)The cost of the books purchased by the author can be deducted from the author's royalty payments but the amount deducted may not exceed $200.00 in any calendarquarter.

(12)The author's royalty payments are processed and mailed each calendar quarter

(13)If deemed necessary by the publisher, the author agrees to make personal appearances for the purpose of promotion.

(14)The payment of personal appearances will be negotiated separately as the need arises.

(15)The publisher may use the author's name, biography, likeness, and selections from the material in connection with the advertising and promotion of the book or the company.

(16)The publisher may edit the manuscript and make changes, or additions as needed for editorial purposes.

(17)The author will be asked to review said changes for content correctness, but the final decision for the content is solely that of the publisher.

(18)The author will notify the publisher of any intent to publish this manuscript in part or in whole in any media or format and an agreement to do so may be formulated at that time.

(19)The author will retain the copyright to this manuscript/book, and must file the appropriate forms and fees with the Federal Copyright Office in Washington, DC. The proper forms and two copies of the Book (as provided in paragraph 9) will be provided by the publisher to the author.

(20)The publisher will file the proper materials and fees to acquire the ISBN and LCCN.

(21)The publisher will retain a five year first World Wide book rights and reprint rights for the same period of time, for this book in any binding, edition, press run or form.

(22)At the end of this five year period, the publisher will have the first option of extending this contract with all the rights contained herein or negotiating a new contract with the author. If the author waives said option or an agreement between the publisher and the author can not be reached the author is free to publish this manuscript by any means at the author's disposal.

(23)The publisher will use every means and effort at the publisher's disposal to assure the manuscript meets with success. However, the publisher states no warranty as to said success.

4)The author assures the publisher that he/she is entitled to grant the rights requested by the publisher for this manuscript as submitted to the publisher.

(25)The author assures the publisher that the manuscript is not under consideration elsewhere.

The above portion of this contract expires five years from the date the first release of this book.

The following portion of this contract has no expiration date and will remain in force for the life of the author.

(26)The author determines the material contained in this manuscript to be accurate.

(27)The author holds the publisher harmless in the event of litigation as a result of a qualified party using the information contained in this manuscript.

(28)The author assures the publisher that the manuscript will not plagiarize another's work.

(29)The author will take due care that the manuscript will not libel, invade the privacy or otherwise violate another's rights.

(30)The author will reimburse the publisher for any loss or expense if the author's agreement to any stipulation above is found to be incorrect in any settlement or judgment.

By my signature set forth below, as the author, I hereby agree to all the stipulations set forth in this document. Furthermore, by initialing each page of this document I attest to reading and understanding each page in its entirety.

I _____ hereby agree to the above statement.

Author:

Address

_____

City _____ State

_____ Zip_____

Phone _____

Social Security or Tax ID _____

By my signature set forth below, as the publisher, I hereby agree to all the stipulations set forth in this document. Furthermore, by initialing each page of this document I attest to reading and understanding each page in its entirety.

I _____ hereby agree to the above. Date _____Publisher: This staff of YOUR PUBLISHER wishes you the best in this endeavor.

REFERENCE MATERIALS AVAILABLE:

Handbook of Magazine Article Writing – Bob Greene

How to sell 75% of your Freelance Writing – Gordon Burgett

How to write a book proposal - - Writer's digest books

Practical tips for Writing Popular Fiction – Roybn Carr

Novel & short story - - Writer's MarketThe Complete Guide to Self Publishing - - Tom & Marilyn Ross

The Writers Digest to Manuscript Format. Writer's Markets

Writer's Digest Magazine

Writing Romances – Rita Gallagher, and Rita Estrada

You can write a romance and get it published – Yvonne Mac Manus

AGENTS.
This is one of those catch twenty-two situations
where you have to have the experience to get the
job, and you need the job to get the experience.
You nearly have to be published to get an Agent
to take you under their wing. Writer's Digest
Magazine, or Writers Markets" can help in this
direction. You can find agents on the West
Coast, but for some reason, the greatest agent
population seems to think the East Coast is the
only place writers sell their work.

When seeking an agent, be careful. Often a
seemingly good agent will come in sheep's
clothing. They will advertise, asking you to send
them a few chapters, in return they may praise
your work, then they will tell you about the reading
fees, the copying fees, the editing fees, etc. etc.

I queried one agent who seemed okay, only to
find out that in the long run, though I am a
published writer, they still expected to make three
thousand dollars from my account before my work
was published with their help. No, the agent I was
communicating with didn't come out and bluntly
say this, but a few questions finally netted the
right person in their office who gave me the scoop
on the way things were done. When you think
about this kind of situation.

The amount of money you might receive from a first printing could end up with nearly all of it going to the agent who is supposed to be working for you, not you working for the agents well being.

Of course there are honest agents, but be prepared for an arduous journey in the search for one that will handle your work. Sometimes one of those editors you've befriended along the way, is the best connection you can have in locating an agent.

Most agents will not handle short fiction. They require longer works. You should also consider that the agent will be, in a sense, your employee. This can help you maintain the right frame of mind while looking for one.

Consider looking at the following Internet sites. Http://www.sfwa.org/beware/agents.html

Suggested Agent Checklist for Authors. The following items are a list of topics for authors to discuss with potential literary agents that they are seeking to do business with. This llst is very similar to those provided by the Association of Authors' Representatives, Inc., 10 Astor Place, 3rd Floor, New York, NY, USA 10003 (212) 3533709.

Upon request, the AAR will send you a listing of the agents who are members of the AAR, and who subscribe to the AAR's Canon of Ethics. Also, a brochure describing some basic information about agents in general, and the AAR in particular. To take advantage of this offer, you must send a SASE #10 envelope with additional postage and a check or money order made payable to the AAR for $7.00, in U.S. currency.

You may feel that of all these questions, some need not to be asked of your agent. If this is the case, be sure to use the ones you feel are pertinent to your situation.

1. Do you own your agency as a sole proprietorship, or are you involved in a partnership, or with a corporation?

2. Are you currently a member of the Association of Authors' Representatives?

3. How long have you been in business as an agent?

4. How many employees do you have?

5. Of the total number of staff employees, how many are agents, and how many are clerical workers?

6. Do you have specialists on hand who specifically handle movie and television rights? Foreign rights? Do you have other subagents or corresponding agents overseas and in Hollywood?

7. Do you represent other authors in my areas of interest?

8. Do you provide editorial input and career guidance for your clients or for me specifically?

9. Who in your agency will actually be handling my work? Will the majority of staff members be familiar with my work, and will they be aware of the status of my business at your agency? Will you oversee or at least keep me current of any work your agency is doing on my behalf?

10. Do you consult with your clients on all offers for their work.

11. What are your procedures and time frames for processing and paying out your client funds?

12. Do you issue 1099 tax forms at the end of each year?

13. What is it you expect of me as a client?

14. Do you issue an agent/author contract? If so, may I review a sample copy of this contract? And if there is a separate section, may I review the language of the agency clause that appears in contracts you negotiate for your clients?

15. How do you inform your clients as to activities on their behalf? Do you regularly send them copies of publishers' rejection letters? Do you

provide them with submission lists and rejection letters on request? Do you regularly, or upon request, send out updated work activity reports?

16. Some agencies sign subsidiary contracts on behalf of their clients to expedite processing. Do you?

17. What are your commissions on the following items(1) basic sales to US publishers, (2) sales of movie and television rights, (3) audio and multimedia rights, (4) British and foreign translation rights?

18. Do you keep different bank accounts separating your author's funds from agency revenue?

19. What are your policies about charging clients for expenses incurred by your agency? Will you list such expenses for me? Do you advance money for such expenses? Do you consult with your clients before advancing certain expenditures? Is there a ceiling on such expenses above which you feel you must consult with your clients?

20. Do you handle the legalities, accounting, public relations and similar professional services, or do these fall outside the normal range of a literary agency's functions?

21. Do you furnish clients upon request with a detailed account of their financial activity, such as gross income, commissions and other deductions, plus net income, for the past year?

22. In the event of your death or disability, or the death or disability of the principal person running the agency, are there provisions in place for the continued handling of my account, and the processing of money due to me, and for the handling of my books and editorial needs?

23. Should we, for whatever reason, part company, what is your policy about handling any unsold subsidiary rights to my work that were reserved to me under the original publishing contracts?

24. Is there a list of Do's and Don'ts provided for your clients that will enable them to help facilitate your agencies work on their behalf?

TRACKING YOUR WORK. ARTICLE or BOOK

Submitted to --------------
Editor's Name--------------
Word Length----------------
Drawings Submitted------
Photos Submitted----------
Accepted---------------------
Published Date-------------
Submission Date----------
Follow up Date------------
Payment Received--------
Market Type----------------
SASE Envelope Number----196
Declined---------------------
ARTICLE or BOOK------------
Submitted to -------------
Editor's Name--------------
Word Length---------------
Drawings Submitted------
Photos Submitted---------.
Accepted-------------------
Published Date----------
Submission Date---------
Follow up Date-----------
Payment Received-----------
SASE Envelope Number---------197
Market Type----------------
Declined-------------------

Tracking your work should become an important work habit. The busier you get in the writing world, the more necessary this becomes. You do not want to receive letters from editors who have read the same article appearing in another publication on at the same time. What happens is that at first you may have to return any funds sent to never sell these editors
any more of your work.

There is no reason to have a return address in the left hand corner, because the address in the center of the envelope is your own. Instead put a number in that corner. This is your tracking number, and don't start out with "1" Start out with a larger number, not extravagant, but something over fifty anyway.

Why big numbers you ask? Because it looks like you're busy to an editor. She knows this number is important to you somehow, and she knows it relates to the work she has in her hand. She doesn't know whether it relates to her file, this article, whether it's just this year, this month, or what, but she knows it has to do with your writing.

WRITING FOR THE WEB

Should you be interested in pursuing this kind of writing, remember that you must hook the reader on the first web page.

If not, odds are they won't follow you from page to page. Also, these pages are not like the written piece of paper, these are the size of your computer screen while you are on the Internet.

Most E-zines will accept unsolicited manuscripts of short stories, and short fiction. Like any magazine, it must be quality prose with good plots and characters. Short stories with an E-zine can be anywhere from twenty five hundred words, to ten thousand words. You will have to inquire which "Genre's are accepted, but most are welcome.

If you send multiple submissions, tell each one of them you have done so, honesty is required in this matter whether an E-zine or magazine. They will require First Electronic Rights, and may or may not offer payment. Submissions may be required in a format like RTF, or Rich Text File. Sometimes an E-zine will accept your story pasted into your E-mail. Always ask their preferences.

When they offer payment, be sure you will get paid in currency rather than promises. Sometimes payment is derived by how many people use the link to your information, or story line. If the link to your work is used it is registered and you are paid by the 'Click.' On the link.

They will require your name, address, E-mail address, telephone number, and a commitment that you are indeed the original author.

Sending your writing resume never hurts your chances of becoming published with any publication, regardless whether its electronic, or paper.

ON LINE PUBLISHERS.
How do you make the decision as to which On Line Publisher to submit work to for consideration? I suggest the following method.

Go to each of the 'On Line' Publishers home page and download their writer's guidelines. After you have these in your hand, read these over and decide which one seems the more professional. You can tell by the questions they ask, and the directions they give the writer to follow.

Once you have singled out one or two of the On Line Publishers, go to their home pages again, and look for their list of current authors. When you have found this information, try to find the section where each author has provided some personal writing background. Often you will find an author who has listed his E-mail address, or a location where he/she can be reached.

Armed with this information feel free to contact the author, and ask for their opinion of the publication they are doing business with. Explain why you want to know, and you might ask about royalty payments. Are they paid on time, does the authors work sell often, do they have any suggestions you might follow, or pitfalls to avoid. As you submit work to an On Line Publisher, you must remember that there is still a slush pile involved, even if it is electronic.

When you will hear about the acceptance of your work will depend on how far down in the pile your work resides.

SAMPLE WEB GUIDELINES FOR WRITERS
Editor@onlineoriginals.com

For a general discussion of our principles for accepting works, please read the introductory pages to the Online Originals site. For a quick look, start with http://www.onlineoriginals.com/howselec.html and follow the questions at the bottom of each page. Please also examine our Works list, peruse the synopses and sample sections, and perhaps read a few of our titles, so that you can assess the kind of works we publish. It is important to note that we can consider only manuscripts which have never been published before in ANY form – including publication on a Web page, in another language or in a privately-financed print edition.

In order for your manuscript to be legible to our qualified readers around the world (who use a wide range of computer systems), Online Originals requests that any proposed 'manuscript' be submitted as a single text only (also called 'ASCII' or 'Plain Text') file attached to an e-mail cover message, and that it follows the formatting guidelines listed below. The aim is to make your text completely free of word processing code (which also saves work at the production stage, should we decide to accept it). We regret that our readers will be unable to recommend manuscripts that do not meet our formatting requirements. However, as far as creativity is concerned, we do our utmost to leave the content and the literary or intellectual approach to you, the writer.

FORMAT
No blank lines between paragraphs, a tabbed indent at the start of each paragraph.

All text left-justified, set to maximum column width (ie, no tables or charts.

No hard returns at line-endings (ie, text runs on within each paragraph).

STYLE
No underlines, italics, bold, different sizes of type, special fonts, or non-ASCII characters (except accented characters in French, German, Italian or Spanish).

Numbers 'one' through 'ten' spelt out, '11' and above as arabic numerals.

HEADINGS
Highest-level headings (eg, for chapters) in ALL CAPS, with three blank lines before the headings and two blank lines after the headings.

Secondary headings (eg, for sections within a chapter) in Initial Caps Only, with one blank line before the heading and one blank line after the heading. tertiary headings (eg, for divisions within a chapter) in ALL CAPS, with one blank line before the heading, and none after (ie, heading directly on top of the text).

Bulletised points numbered as 1/ 2/ 3/ with two word spaces after the slash and each bullet formatted as a separate paragraph.

For un-headed divisions in any text, use * * *, left-justified, with one blank line before, and one blank line after.

NOTES Footnotes in text marked as (1), (2), etc. with one word   space before; footnotes themselves at the end of the entire text, not at the end of chapters.

PUNCTUATION
Semi-quote marks to contain names of books, journals, etc, using straight-up-and-down style, not curled.

Double-quote marks to contain conversation, quotations, etc, using straight-up-and-down style, not curled.

Apostrophes in strait-up-and-down style, not curled.

Two adjacent hyphens – instead of long dash
References or reference-footnotes shown as
Author, 'Title', City: Publisher, year, pages
numbers.

No full stops (Periods) used in abbreviations,
initials,(eg, cm, CIA, Mr)

No use of & £, \, |,@, *, %, +, =, etc, since many
symbols have functional uses on the World Wide
Web; spell out your meanings (eg, pounds
Sterling, percent, plus, equals) Historical periods
written as 1800s, 1700s etc with no apostrophe

When listing three or more items, place a comma
before the final 'and'

Use one word space (not two, as in typing)
between sentences

Do not put a word space before a ! or ? When
using a series of full stops (periods) to indicate
continuing thoughts or text, use only three and put
one word space on either side, like this . . .

Turn off all automatic hyphenation on your word
processor and do not split a word over two lines
(manually-hyphenated words in the middle of lines
are allowed of course)

Thank you for following these guidelines. Please
also do a complete 'spell check' of your work
before you send it. And please when you send the

file to us by e-mail, put the title of the work in the e-mail subject line, as this helps hugely in our keeping track of the submissions. In terms of writing style, here's a little casual advice on our preferences. For fiction and drama, nearly anything goes except gratuitous profanity, extreme violence or highly-explicit obscenity. For non-fiction, you should keep in mind that your work will be read across the world.

For an internationally-acceptable style of English non-fiction, we tend to consult 'Oxford English' for grammar and 'The Economist style Guide' for clarity. The latter recommends among other principles, George Orwell's six elementary rules: (1)Never use a metaphor, simile or other figure of speech which you are used to seeing or hearing.

Never use a long word where a short word will do;

If it is possible to cut out a word, always cut it out;

Never use the passive where you can use the active.

Never use a foreign phrase, a scientific word or a jargon word if you can think of an everyday English equivalent; (6)Break any of these rules sooner than say anything outright barbarous. (Politics and the English Language', 1946) Once again we mention these guidelines only to indicate our preferences, not to tell you how you should write.

When we receive your work, it goes by e-mail to our qualified readers – who specialize in fiction or non-fiction or drama – based in Europe, North America and Australia. We respond with specific comments and a "yes' or 'no' as soon as the readers are finished, usually in a few months. (Sorry if this seems a long time. Although technology can speed up communications and transactions, it does nothing to speed up reading and thinking.

Moreover, all our readers work on a voluntary basis.) If we say 'yes' we will send an e-mail and Adobe Acrobat PDF contract for you to print out and sign, and ask additional information such as biography, synopsis, etc. During digital production in preparation for publication on the Web, we rigorously sub-edit for syntax, grammar, punctuation, spelling, and clarity of communication. Incidentally, we are authorized to assign ISBN numbers to our published works.

There is no cost to the author in publishing a work with Online Originals; indeed, we pay the authors royalties of 50 percent. But we hope that authors will support the enterprise by spreading the word about Online Originals to people they know.

Thank you again for your enquiry.

With best wishes.
Editor
Online Originals

'GLOSSARY'
Writer's Market

Advance. This is money the publisher pays the author before the book is published. This money is repaid to the publisher by the royalties earned.

Advertorial. This is an advertisement that appears to be an editorial article.

Agent. A liaison between a writer, and an editor, or publisher. An agent usually markets the writer's work.

All rights. The publisher purchases all of the writer's rights, normally forever.

Anthology. A collection of various writings.

Assignment. An article an editor asks a writer to produce for an agreed upon price.

Auction. Something every writer hopes happens to them. A situation where a manuscript looks so promising that several publications want to purchase the material.

Avant-garde. Work that is very inventive in style, and difficult to write.

B&W. Black and white photographs.

Backlist. A list of books that a publisher has printed, but not in the current season.

Belles lettres. Fine literary writing, more for fun reading, than informative, or instructive.

Bimonthly. Published every other month.

Bio. Yes, of course, information about the writer.

Biweekly. Published every two weeks.

Blog. A method of communicating ones thoughts to anyone at any time, on the internet.

Boilerplate. A standard contract. One that has been well established, but is often changed to suit the conditions.

Book packager. Someone who does all the work to put a book together. Including the writing, marketing, etc. Then sells the book to a publisher.

Business size envelope. A #10 size.

Byline. The writer's name as it appears on a published work.

Category fiction. A label attached to various types of fiction.

CD-ROM. A compact disk, which is read by electronic devices, and can contain a huge amount of data.

Chapbook. A small booklet, usually ballads, stories, or poetry.

Clean copy. A manuscript that is free of wrinkles, smudges, crossed out words, and error free.

Clips. Copies, or Samples of your work from previous publications.

Coffee table book. An oversized book containing a great deal of illustrations.

Column inch. The amount of space in one column inch of typeset.

Commercial novels. Novels many people read, such as romance, mystery, western, or known as 'Genres'.

Commissioned work. The same as 'Assignment'.

Concept. A summary of a screenplay, or teleplay.

Contact sheet. Photographic paper, which often contains an entire roll of film on an uncut sheet of paper.

Contributors copies. Copies of the work sent to the writer.

Cooperative publishing. This is the same as co-publishing.

Co-publishing. This is an agreement between the writer, and the publisher as to costs of publishing the work.

Copyediting. Checking a manuscript for its punctuation, grammar, and printing style.

Copyright. A method of protecting the authors work.

Cover letter. A letter describing the work it accompanies, used with a book, or manuscript.

Creative nonfiction. Nonfictional writing that uses an innovative approach to the subject and creative language.

CV. Curriculum vita, A brief list of the authors accomplishments, and qualifications.

Derivative works. A previously written work that has undergone a translation, adapted, abridged, condensed, annotated, or altered from its original form.

Desktop publishing. A method of publishing using a desktop computer system.

Disk. A storage device for computer data.

Docudrama. Film fiction of recent newsmaking events.

Dot-matrix. Printed type that is composed of small dots of ink.

Editor in Chief
The person in charge of the editorial part of the magazine. Except on magazines with very small staffs. The editor in chief may not work directly

with many writers, especially new ones.
Sometimes though, he, or she is the best person to address a query to, since it's likely to be passed on to the appropriate editor.

Executive Editor
Another editor who may not work directly with many writers but may instead manage other editors.

Managing Editor
Often an editor in charge of getting the magazine out on schedule. Some managing editors work with freelance writers, but most don't.
Articles Editor Is just about what it sounds like. The articles editor, if the magazine has one, is often the best person to send your work, or query to.

Senior Editor, Associate Editor, Assistant Editor, etc.
Various degrees of editors who may, or may not work with freelance writers. Sometimes an editor who is low on the masthead will be a good bet to contact. Because he, or she, may take more personal interest in you than more experienced editors who are already working with as many writers as they can handle.

Eclectic. Publication features a variety of different writing styles of genres.

Electronic submissions. Something you submit by modem, or disk.

El-hi. Elementary high school.

E-mail. Data you write on a computer and send via the electronic network.

Epigram. A short, witty, paradoxical saying.

Epistolary. Opening a story with letters, journals, or diary entries.

Erotica. Fiction or art, that is sexually orientated.

Experimental. See Avante garde.

Fair use. A method of using work from copyrighted works without infringing on the original work.

Fax. A method of sending documents over telephone lines.

Feature. A humane interest story, rather than news.

Filler. A short story used to fill a space in a publication.

First North American rights. The permission given a publication to publish an authors work the first time in the USA

Formula story. A predictable plot story line.

Frontlist. A list of books a publisher has in current publication.

Galleys. A first version of a manuscript, not yet published.

Genre. A classification of story lines, such as mystery, romance, science fiction, etc.

Ghostwriter. A writer who writes another persons story.

Gift book. Often a small book intended to be given as a gift.

Glossy. A black and white photo with a shiny surface.

Gothic novel. Normally a historic novel, such as life in castles, mansions, beautiful young women, and heroic men.

Graphic novel. Illustrated stories, such as comics, or?

Flash drive. A magnetic storage device that can hold all of the information you might keep on your computer hard drive.

Hard copy. A printed version of an author's work.

Hardware. The mechanical components of a computer system.

High-lo. Generally written for adults with high interest, but low reading abilities.

Home page. The first page of an World Wide Web page.

Honorarium. A small payment, or copies with a writer's byline.

How-to. Manuscripts produced to give instructions on how someone can accomplish a task.

Hypertext. A group of words that linked to another document.

Illustrations. This can be art work, drawings, photographs, engravings, and usually separate from the manuscript.

Imprint. Names applied to a publishers different line of books.

Interactive. Computer generated actions according to information the user provides.

Interactive fiction. Software formats which take direction depending upon the users input. The story structure is determined by the way the writer writes.

Internet. A world wide network of computer supplied information.

Invasion of privacy. Writing about a person without their permission to do so.

Kill fee. A payment for work assigned, but subsequently canceled.

Lead time. The time between the purchase of a manuscript, and the time it is published.

Letter-quality. A computer printout that looks as if it is typewritten.

Libel. A published accusation or statement, that sheds unfair light upon another individual.

List royalty. Royalties paid depending upon the marketed value of a manuscript.

Literary fiction. Serious, intelligent fiction.

Little magazine. A publication of limited circulation.

LORT. Means League of Resident Theaters.

Magalog. Mail order catalog with how-to articles pertaining to their products.

Mainstream fiction. This kind of fiction falls outside the normal genre's such as mystery, romance, science fiction, etc.

Mass market. Nonspecialized books directed toward a large audience. Smaller and cheaper than paper backs. Often found in supermarkets, and drug stores etc.

Mast Head When a magazine has a 'Mast Head,' it is a list of its staff. However not all magazines have a Mast Head list.

Microcomputer. Small computers such as handheld, notebooks, and other personal devices.

Midlist. Publications that are not expected to produce large sales. These are mainstream, usually written by unknown writers.

Model releases. A paper signed by anyone involved in a photograph giving the photographer permission to use it for some specific purpose.

Modem. An electronic device used to transmit data from one location to another.

Monograph. A detailed study of any single subject.

Multi-media. The ability to integrating sound, photos, animation, and video together.

Multiple submissions. Generally this is associated with sending more than one copy of your work to several editors at the same time.

Narrative nonfiction. A narrative presentation of actual events.

Narrative poem. Poetry that tells a story.

Net royalty. Royalties paid on money earned after discounts, special sales, returns etc.

Network. Computers that are linked electronically togethrer.

New Age. These are topics that at one time seemed far fetched, but are now gaining wider audience acceptance.

Newsbreak. A late breaking story added to the newspaper, magazine, or newscast.

NLQ. Near Letter Quality printout required by some editors.

Novella. A short novel, or narrative story. A tale. 7,500 to 40,000 words.

Novelette. A short novel, or a long story. 7,000 to 25,000 words.

Novelization. A novel created from a script of a movie.

Offprint. Copies of an author's work taken 'out of issue' before the magazine is given to the author in lieu of monetary payment.

On spec. An editor is interested in seeing the finished product, but is not under obligation to purchase the work.

One-shot, or one time feature. A single feature story for a syndicate to sell.

One-time rights. Work that a writer has offered for sale one time only.

Online. Using a telephone line for transmitting data from one location to another.

Online service. This provides a computer user with the ability to access the Internet, and E-mail usage.

Outline. A summery of a book's contents. Usually 5–15 double spaced pages. Such as chapter headings with a sentence or two of description.

Over-the-transom. A term used by editors for unsolicited work by a freelance writer.

Package sale. An editor buys a package of photos, manuscript, and pays for them with one check.

Page rate. An amount paid for each page of published work.

Parallel submission. Using the same basic information in different manners for different publications at the same time.

Parody. The conscious imitation of work, usually with the intention to make fun of, or to ridicule the work.

Payment on publication. The writer doesn't get paid for the work until it is published.

Pen name. The use of a name other than your legal name on articles or stories when you wish to remain anonymous. Also known as a pseudonym.

Photo feature. A story line based on photographs rather than on text.

Plagiarism. Passing off the work of others, as if it were your own.

Potboiler. Writing projects a writer produces while working on some other major work, such as a lengthy book. How-to, short stories, fill this need.

Proofreading. Requires a close reading of material to find and correct errors in the work before publication.

Proposal. A summery of a book submitted to a publisher for consideration.

Proscenium. The portion of the stage right in front of the curtain.

Prospectus. A preliminary description of a book or article.

Pseudonym. The use of a name other than your legal name on articles or stories when you wish to remain anonymous. Also known as a pen name.

Public domain. Material that has never been copyrighted, or is out of copy right.

Query. A letter to an editor, which is written to entice the editor in purchasing the work.

Release. The selling of an idea that is wholly owned by oneself.

Remainders. Copies of a book that can be purchased at a reduced cost from the publisher. Seldom is a royalty paid on the sale of remainders.

Reporting time. A time period where the editor gets back to an author about a query or manuscript.

Reprint rights. Usually rights that the publisher wants. This is in case the book, or? Does well on the market.

Round-up article. Comments from, or interviews with celebrities, or experts on a particular theme.

Royalties, standard hardcover book. Usually 10% on the first 5,000 copies, 12 ½ % percent on the next 5,000 copies.

Royalties, standard mass paperback books. 4 to 8% of the retail price on the first 150,000 copies sold.

Royalties, standard trade paperback. No less than 6% of list price on the first 20,000 copies; 7 ½% thereafter.

Royalties, E-zines. It is not unusual to receive 50% of the market price.

Scanning. A method of reading the work by a computer, and converted into workable text, or material.

Screenplay. Script for a film intended to be shown in theaters.

Second rights. This is selling the story again and again, unchanged from its original form, and after it has been sold the first time for first rights.

Self-publishing. You pay for the manufacture, the marketing, and you keep all the money.

Semimonthly. Published twice a month.

Semiweekly. Published twice a week.

Serial. Published periodically, such as a newspaper.

Sidebar. A small feature presented as a companion to another longer article. Generally information pertinent to the article, but not used in the article.

Similar submissions. Using the same basic information in different manners for different publications at the same time.

Simultaneous submissions. Sending the same work to several editors at the same time. Be sure to tell them you are doing so.

Slant. The method of writing the material for a specific area, or audience.

Slice-of-life vignette. A short piece of fiction intended to show an interesting piece of everyday life.

Slides. Transparent photos for editors to consider using.

Slush pile. A stack of unsolicited manuscripts received by a publication.

Preferred slush pile. A stack of known writers who regularly submit work to a publication.

Sophomore Jinx. It is the seeming inability to write another novel after just completing, and publishing the first one.

Software. Programs a user loads into a computer system. Such as a word processor program.

Speculation. An agreement that an editor will look at an authors work with no promise of its being used.

Style. The way something is written.

Subsidiary rights. All those rights except those included in a book contract.

Subsidy publisher. A book publisher who constructs the book for the writer. The writer covers all costs.

Synopsis. A brief summary of a manuscript, condensed into a few pages, single spaced.

Tabloid. A small style of newspaper.

Tagline. A caption for a photo, or comment added to a filler.

Tearsheet. A page or sheet of printed material containing the author's work.

Teleplay. A play written for, or performed on television.

TOC. Table of Contents.

Trade. Special interest books directed toward the lay person.

Transparencies. Positive color slides, not a finished photo.

Treatment. Synopsis of a television, or film script.

Unsolicited manuscript. Something a writer sends to an editor, without the editor asking to see the material.

User friendly. Computer software programs that are easy to use.

Vanity publisher. A book publisher who constructs the book for the writer. The writer covers all costs.

Word Processor. A computer program that allows the user to write, and make easy corrections to that work. Something every writer should have.

World Wide Web. An Internet access to information.

Work-for-hire. A writer who produces written work for a publication and gets paid for it. This writer does not own the copyright.
YA. Young adults books.

Itchy Feet Publications
mgn.editor@gmail.com
Other books written by Donald Boone

WRITING TO PUBLISH
Becoming a published writer is a plateau most writers wish
to attain. The trick to becoming successful, is in learning
what is required to catch the editor's eye. Once you cross
over the threshold of becoming published, it does get easier.
This book is comprised of information you should find useful
in helping you to attain the status of success in a difficult
world of words.
ISBN 1-882896-19-X
EAN 978-1-882898-19-6
Ebook 978-1-882896-40-0

THE CHESS SET
In the past, chess sets were completely custom made. No
two were alike. A few may have been pieces of tree
branches, or perhaps rocks and sea shells, things that only
the players understood what function they served. A few
were elaborate, and very, very expensive. This story is about
a chess set that not only cost its owner a King's ransom, it
also instructed the owner on the best possible moves to
make. Information that is available yet today.
ISBN 1-882896-18-1
EAN 978-1-882896-18-9
Ebook 978-1-882896-39-4

CHESS HISTORIES & MYSTERIES
The stories you'll read in this book have, as a rule, some line
of history involved. So take a tour through the past and
pretend you were there.
E book 9781882896264
ISNB 1-882896-17-3
EAN 978-1-882896-17-2

CHESS STORIES THROUGH THE AGES
This book, 'Chess Stories Through The Ages,' contains
stories that have been passed from one generation to the
next down through history. From why 'White moves first, and
an unknown story of 'Helen of Troy, found in, 'The Sacrificed
Trojan Horse.'
E book 9781882896271
ISBN 1-882896-10-6
EAN 978-1882896-10-3

THOSE WHO PLAY CHESS
Knowing how your opponent plays chess, his or her favorite
pieces and their quirks, are a definite advantage to you in
this game. Especially if you play in tournaments. This book
will provide you with information on them as individuals, and
that of their personalities. You will also find lists of historical
players with the same kinds of individualism's and
personalities to help guide you in your defense at the table.
E book 9781882896370
ISBN 1-882896-11-4
EAN 978 -1-882896 -11-0

THE CHESS GAME
Having lost a huge sum in prize money due to an oversight
in a championship chess game, he became a revenge killer.
He spelled it out for his opponents during his killing spree.
You will see the connection as you read this story.
E book 9781882896349
ISBN 1-882896-13-0
EAN 978-1882896-13-4

THE CHESS COACH
Becoming one is easy, and it can be
very rewarding. If you play the game
and have time on your hands, consider
becoming a chess coach.
E book 9781882896356
ISBN 1-882896-08-4
EAN 978-1882896-08-0

CHOOSING LOVERS
Why spend years with the wrong lover.
Find the one that best suits your needs
and enjoy freedom from sexual hunger.
E book 9781882896288
ISBN 1-882896-04-1
EAN 978-1-882896-04-2

CYCLES & RHYTHMS of INTRIGUE
Most of life, if not all of it, contains cycles.
From the birth of any event it will find
its natural rhythm and follow it to the
end. Is life fated, read the answer in this
book.
E book 9781882896295
ISBN 1-882896-07-6
EAN 978-1-882896-07-3

THE SEA PILOT
In this age of sailing vessels, we no longer fear sailing over
the edge of the flat world, and we find our way with compass
and chronometer. This was not so when this story took
place.
E book 9781882896363
ISBN 1-882896-09-2
EAN 978-1-882896-09-7

IMPACT
Meteors have been haunting mankind since the beginning of
mankind, and they still do. This story is about one of those
celestial bodies that does not miss the earth on its path
around our sun. Like meteorites of the past, the damage it
causes when it strikes the earths surface, is devastating.
However, many survive and this story is about how one
group came together to get through the worst of the affects.

E book 9781882896301
ISBN 1-882896-12-2
EAN 978-1-882896-12-7

WELCOME ABOARD
When those who have lived around the water, and their day
comes to an end, it is time to relax. Whether they are lying in
a Vee birth, or on a cushion in the cockpit of a boat. Perhaps
even a bed ashore. It doesn't matter as they frequently have
an abundance of time. To fill the time they read and let the
stories unfold in their mind's as the hours pass by. This book
is comprised of stories that take place in this world. A place
where you meet life on its terms.

E book 9781882896387
ISBN 1-882896-03-3
EAN 978-1-882896-03-5

SEXUAL HAPPINESS
Sexual happiness is one of the most important things to
happen in your life. This book is designed to help you look
for the correct person to have in your life. This kind of search
is seldom preformed, but it should be the case in every
relationship. Be honest with yourself about your own needs,
then use this book to find the best lover to fill your own life.

E book 9781882896332
ISBN 1-882896-16-5
EAN 978-1-882896-16-5

LOST ISLAND

Because of his beliefs about those in power, and of the church, he'd been banned to live a life at sea. After four years of not stepping ashore, he took a chance on escape. He'd waited two years just to get near this lost Island again. An Island that he did not even know if he could survive on it, but feeling it was better than his current life. A bribe and the Captain's skiff helped him escape the ship, but only to find himself fighting for his life in a violent storm at sea. To hid wonderment, the Island became a place of haven, and one of pleasure as well. A place unknown to the rest of the world.

E book 9781882896325
ISBN 1-882896-15-7
EAN 978-1-882896-15-8

LIVING ABOARD PROJECTS

Moving onboard a boat is when you find there are things that need to be changed to make life aboard better and more comfortable. This book has 43 projects plus other useful information you might find of interest to helping your easement into life aboard, and those who might be joining you.

E book 9781882896318
ISBN 1-882896-02-5
EAN 978-1-882896-02-8

www.ingramcontent.com/pod-product-compliance
Lightning Source LLC
Chambersburg PA
CBHW051819090426
42736CB00011B/1555